T0195758

Is Jesus God?

Third Edition

Shirley Holmes-Sulton

Order this book online at www.trafford.com
or email orders@trafford.com

Most Trafford titles are also available at major online book retailers.

© Copyright 2014 Shirley Holmes-Sulton.
All rights reserved. No part of this publication may be reproduced, stored in a retrieval
system, or transmitted, in any form or by any means, electronic, mechanical, photocopying,
recording, or otherwise, without the written prior permission of the author.

Scripture taken from the Holy Bible, Today's New International Version™ TNIV®
Copyright © 2001, 2005 by International Bible Society®. All rights reserved worldwide.

Print information available on the last page.

ISBN: 978-1-4907-3049-3 (sc)
ISBN: 978-1-4907-3047-9 (hc)
ISBN: 978-1-4907-3048-6 (e)

Library of Congress Control Number: 2014904551

Because of the dynamic nature of the Internet, any web addresses or links contained in
this book may have changed since publication and may no longer be valid. The views
expressed in this work are solely those of the author and do not necessarily reflect the
views of the publisher, and the publisher hereby disclaims any responsibility for them.

Any people depicted in stock imagery provided by Thinkstock are models,
and such images are being used for illustrative purposes only.
Certain stock imagery © Thinkstock.

Trafford rev. 04/09/2015

 www.trafford.com

North America & international
toll-free: 1 888 232 4444 (USA & Canada)
fax: 812 355 4082

CONTENTS

PREFACE

This book is based on scriptures. In order for God to reveal Himself to us through scriptures (His Word), we must study them daily. Many times we read the Word of God, but we need to study it. We must meditate both day and night on it. One writer said, "I meditate on the Word of God more than the necessary food for my body." Whatever you practice is what you become. To be a child of God, we must study His Word and write it upon the tables of our heart as Moses in **Deuteronomy 6:7-9** said. "You shall teach them diligently unto your children, and shall talk of them when you sit in your house, when you walked by the way and when you rises up. You shall bind them for a sign upon your hand, and they shall be as frontlets between your eyes. You shall write them upon the post of your house, and on your gates." I remember my daughter saying, at the age of eight, "Mommy, my teacher said practice makes perfect." If we let God be priority in our lives, and in our conversations, then we will be able to work towards our perfection in Him; everything about us will be holy. The Word said to be Holy, for He is Holy, let your conversations be Holy. The Bible admonishes us to seek God first, and train our children to seek Him also. Yes, teach and train them about God while they are young. We should train them to memorize the Word, scriptures such as **Psalms 23**, the Lord's Prayer **Matthew 6:6-13**, as well as living examples of how to pray and how to live. If we do the will of God in teaching our children, we will have less crime, divorce, murders, stealing and falling away from the love of God. "My people are destroyed for the lack of knowledge.." Knowledge begins before birth, through birth, and continues on after birth.

I'm convinced that people are not and have not studied their Bible. They rely on what they are told by others and once a week in Sunday services or television ministries. I remember asking different leaders and lay people concerning Jesus Christ only, or Jesus Christ as the Son of God, His Father (God) and the Holy Ghost for almost 40 years. That's because I hadn't studied properly. Therefore, I was limited in the knowledge of the scriptures. I was only familiar with Genesis, Isaiah, and III John, concerning Jesus being the Son of God. But God has taken me on a tour through the Bible, and the trip is unexplainable. I held fast to scriptures that told me "God never change." He said before one jot or title of my Word pass away, heaven and earth shall pass away." God also tells us "Not to add nor take away from His Word." It seems to me that the Bible plainly states that there are three (3) that bear witness in heaven and three (3) on earth. Should we dispute God's Word? God said let us make man in our image. We have the words *us* and *our* as plural pronouns. Plurals are more than one.

During my early twenties, I recall trying to figure out how people were so blind to God's Word, although I was limited too, but what I knew I knew. My children's father was "Jesus only," which brought about many fruitless discussions. One of the questions was, "How could God sit on His own right-hand side. Years later God opened my eyes to Brother Matthew and John.

There is a portion of scripture in Psalms that states Jesus will sit on the right hand of his Father and cause his enemy to be his footstool. At my first discovery of this scripture, I tried calling certain people to share the excitement of it. However, no one answered their phone, so I called to share it with my mother. Next, I called my youngest offspring in Atlanta, Georgia. I suppose he thought a huge financial blessing came through. In my excitement, I expressed the wonderful revelation. God had opened my spiritual eyes and taught me His wonderful Word. In studying the Word, God will begin to reveal and increase our spiritual awareness. I can say without any doubt that God the Father, Lord of Lords, has given all power to His Son, Jesus Christ, and that His Son (Jesus) is sitting on his (God) right hand.

God is truly great and worthy to be praised. Here's the portion of scripture that blew my mind one morning, found in both the Old and New Testaments. It states, "How then does David in spirit call Him

Lord, saying the Lord said unto my Lord, sit thou on my right hand, till I make your enemies thy footstool?" Not knowing that Jesus Christ posed this same question to the Pharisees, I often wondered myself, concerning the scriptures of Jesus Christ sitting on the right hand of His Father. This portion of scripture bears a little more in-depth studying. Notice that it read, "How then does David in spirit call Him Lord, saying the Lord said unto my Lord, sit thou on my right hand, till I make your enemies thy footstool?" Lord said unto my Lord (God speaking to His Son, Jesus Christ). This is so blessed and divine.

If we really want to know who Jesus Christ is, He will reveal Himself to us. All we have to do is have that desire and faith of a mustard seed. He will open our eyes as He continues to open mine daily.

Each writer of the Gospel have their own writing style of who Jesus Christ is, and each one grasps and excites me more as my knowledge and faith continues to increase in God's Word. Matthew recorded Jesus Christ posing a question to the Pharisees: "What think ye of Christ?" This is a question posed to His disciples as well. To me this is a very important question, but the answer is as equally important.

During my fifties, I diligently began to study God's Word in depth. The more I studied, the more He opened my eyes to Himself and His Son Jesus Christ, word for word and scripture upon scripture. The Holy Spirit guided me in naming the first two books, **"Everybody Ought To Know Who Jesus Is."** Now, ten years later, in my third book, He led me to rename it, **"Is Jesus God?"**

I maintain that the real thing is to know Him in our hearts, minds and souls. Praise God. Amen. Thy Word have I hid in my heart, that I might not sin against God.

Acknowledgements

God our Father and Jesus Christ His Son, most of all, is to be acknowledged first. For it is God who gave me the knowledge and wisdom to let the people know that Jesus Christ is who He says He is. Don't change nor take away from my Word, says the Lord God. Don't try to be a mystery solver, nor the great I am, for it is hidden to the blind, yet so plain that a fool cannot error. For the Word of God says His thoughts are not our thoughts, nor His ways our ways.

This book is dedicated to my mother, Minnie Lee Martin-Pinder. She was alive during my first two books, but is no longer here with us. She was my greatest inspiration. Thank you mom for the understanding and encouragement you provided me with. Mother Martin-Pinder had unshaken faith that Jesus Christ is the Son of God.

In memory to Elder Timothy Holmes Sr., who was also alive during the first two books, and our four wonderful offsprings, Tamar, Timothy, Terry and Tyrone Holmes.

May God richly pour out His spiritual blessings out upon, my dad Nathaniel James, my siblings Minnie Reese and Donald James, inlaws, all of my children, grandchildren, great grandchildren, spiritual children, adopted children, nieces, nephews, especially Ronnie Reese who did the Editing for me, guard children, saints and their children, friends and their children, neighbors, acquaintances and all of my enemies.

The book would never be complete without mentioning my former pastor and great teacher Elder and Pastor Author W. Goins who passed on at a ripe old viable age of 100. He was the first to bring our attention to Genesis, where the scriptures states; "Let us make man," I can yet hear him, as he would say "us" is plural, and means more than one.

Cheers to my late husband, Bishop Leon Sulton, who was there for me in all of my endeavors and my greatest supporter on this side of heaven.

HISTORY OF ORIGINS

This is the third book in my attempt to share with the world who Jesus is. The first two editions were named "Everybody Ought To Know Who Jesus Is". I renamed the third edition to "Is Jesus God?", changing the title, not the content. My first book was written, beginning with the New Testament book of John. John excited me so much, I just wanted to take a running start and spread the Good News! Years before I conceived writing a book, I dealt with fragments of scripture, such as II John 5:7, and III John. God opened my spiritual eye, gave me more understanding, and placed in my heart to write the second book, with the Old first and then the New. The second book was more of a scripture reference text. And now the third book is a combination of the first two, beginning with Genesis, mixed in with the New Testament and ending in Revelation.

This book came out of the desire to shed some light on God's Word as to whom God is, and His Son Jesus Christ. So many have different views of whom Jesus and God are. I never knew that Christians could be so divided in beliefs, even in the same home, on this one topic. During the early years of my marriage, I sought answers to this worldwide controversy. I prayed and asked different people about their beliefs. I wanted to know if Jesus and God were the same one person. I knew that they were both in agreement, therefore they are one, but during our discussions it would be stated that it is not three, but one. I was puzzled at this point because the Bible plainly states three. I prayed and asked God to show me His Word and Truth. The Lord God took me to I John 5:7. I recommend everyone read the entire fifth Chapter of I John. I tried relentlessly to figure the math or English out, because the Scriptures state that three bear witness in heaven and three in the earth.

Another portion of scripture is that Jesus sits on the right-hand side of His Father. How can one twist that around? I feel that some want to be the great I am, or maybe change it enough to start a new organization and followers. Whatever the reasons are, they have to answer to God for themselves. I do know that the scriptures tell us not to add nor take away from the Word of God. It seems to me since Jesus said His Father sent Him, why can't we believe Him at His Word? Why then do we try to make it a great mystery? Well, it is a mystery to those that it hasn't been revealed to.

What I've done is to search the scriptures under the anointing of the Holy Ghost and compiled them together from Genesis to Revelation, so everyone will know that Jesus Christ is the Son of the true and living God.

All who read this book will be blessed spiritually. Eyes will be opened and ears unstopped. You will not be the same again, your life will began to change and you will have a better understanding of that great question, **"Is Jesus God?"** Remember Jesus asked His disciples that same age-old question, "Who do you say that I am?" Peter answered, "Thou are the Christ, the Son of the True and Living God." Jesus Christ's reply was, "You are blessed, Simon Bar-Jona: because flesh and blood did reveal it to you, but my Father, which is in heaven." **Matthew 16:13-17.**

Note: ***Denotes scripture text from The Bible Experience.

Remember three things, God can't lie, God can't die and God can't sin.

IS JESUS GOD?
IN
THE OLD TESTAMENT

CHAPTER I

Jesus Christ the Word of God

God's Son Revealed in Scripture

Many contend that Jesus and God are the same person, and others believe that Jesus is the Son of God. While others say that we worship three Gods, we don't, we worship the one and only true and living God. But in Him is God the Father, God the Son and God the Holy Spirit. God is the God of all. One Lord, one Faith and one Baptism. God is a spirit. The attributes of God are His Word (Jesus) and the Holy Spirit. We will search the scriptures and let God walk us into the truth. The question is, "Is Jesus God?" Jesus asked his disciples this same question. He wanted to know what the people were saying about him as well as themselves. They expressed to him that, some called him John the Baptist, Elias, Jeremias and some a prophet. Jesus insisted on knowing how they felt, so he probed further. "Ok, but, whom do you say that I am?" Peter jumped up and said, "You are Jesus Christ, the Son of the living God." Jesus said, "Yes but, you didn't get this on your own, my Father in heaven has revealed it to you." **Matthew 16:13-19.**

In the Old Testament, the first Adam, God spoke and cursed the people because of their sin. In the New Testament, the second Adam, God spoke and blessed the people, with grace, mercy and forgiveness of sin through our Lord and Savior Jesus Christ.

I heard a renowned TV personality in one breath say one thing, and in the next, contradict herself. She said God came down Himself, and in the next sentence, she said that God sent His Son Jesus. Now which one is it? Did God send His Son Jesus Christ, or did God come down Himself? We fail to understand that God manifested His Word through His Son Jesus Christ. One important fact is that God didn't come down Himself, He sent His Son Jesus Christ out from Himself. One portion of the scriptures tells us that Jesus was in the bosom of God. God can't lie; neither can He die. Jesus didn't and couldn't lie, but he certainly died. I don't want to leave him there dead, because he rose again. That gives me hope that when I die this natural death I'm going to rise again, too.

The Old Testament conceals and the New Testament reveals who Jesus Christ is. Now when we speak, our words are our bond, when God speaks, His Word is His Son. We cannot separate our words from ourselves. But God allowed the Holy Ghost and His holy Word to emanate from Him so that we could be redeemed through His Word (Jesus Christ) and filled with His Holy Spirit. Christ came out of the bosom of God. We cannot see God Himself, only Jesus Christ has seen Him, because he came out from Him. **John 1:18.** But we can have an experience with Him through His Word and the Holy Spirit. That is why the scripture says the Word was God, and the Word was with God. And the Word is God, which emanates from Him.

I don't like describing this in such an elementary way, but I want to be understood. There are three attributes of God, three that bear witness on earth and three parts to man. The three attributes of God are the Father, the Word, and the Holy Ghost. The three that bear witness on earth are Holy Spirit the keeping power, water baptism and the blood. The three parts of man are mind, body and soul. God wants all three parts of us to be connected with Him. Therefore if we get Jesus Christ into us (the Word), we have God. From the beginning, God's plan was to impute His Word into us, so He sent His Son Jesus Christ to us in the New Testament. God speaks about His Son throughout the Old Testament. He gives us a glimpse of Jesus in Genesis and a full view in Isaiah on throughout Revelation. In the Old Testament, God spoke His Word to us through His prophets. In the New Testament, He releases the full knowledge of who God is through His Son, Jesus Christ. The New Testament made it possible for the Word to enter us. It searches, cleanse and change us; it takes out corruption and impurities which once were, and now no more, since Jesus entered our lives. For we are redeemed (bought back), washed in the blood of the lamb. In the Old Testament, a lamb was an animal; in the New Testament, Jesus is the Lamb—the Lamb of God. When God spoke in the Old Testament, they didn't question who he was. They knew who he was. Not only did they know who He was, but for the most part, they answered to His call or voice.

For example, God came down in the cool of the day to speak with Adam and Eve. As God begin to question them, Adam's reply was, "I heard thy voice in the garden and was afraid because I was naked: and I hid myself." Now this indicates a few things to me. One, Adam and Eve had regular communication with God and two, they recognized and knew who God was, and they knew His voice. Only if we would recognize, know, listen and obey His voice today, our spiritual life would be more in depth with Him because He is constantly speaking to all of us. **Genesis 3:8-13.** Later, in the same chapter, Jesus Christ and God are holding a conversation with each other. The Lord God said, "Behold, the man is becoming as one of us, to know good and evil." Without going any further, "one of us" means one of US. Who are they? God the Father, and Jesus Christ, the Son. I'm convinced that God is yet speaking to us. But Satan has our ears stopped up. Why wouldn't He yet be speaking to us? When the New Testament declares that, "He that has an ear, let him hear." We should listen with both our outer and inner ears. What is the inner ear? It's our spiritual ear.

I feel led to include a few more Bible personalities or prophets that God spoke with. I want you to note that none of the prophets questioned the voice of God in the Old Testament. They recognized His voice. For example, God spoke to Cain when he killed his brother Abel. He asked Abel the where about of brother? Cain's answer was, "I don't know, I'm not his keeper, so why are you asking me?" **Genesis 4:9.** Not a good answer. Cain lied, but yet there was communication between the two of them. Then there was Noah. When God saw how corrupt the world had become, He instructed Noah to build an ark so He could destroy and put an end to all the corruption, violence and sinful people that was in the world. **Genesis 6:13-14.** Another example of God's communication is with his prophet Abraham. First he summons him to leave his country and move away from his kinfolk. Next, God promised to make him a great nation. **Genesis 12:1-2.** Later we see where God spoke to Jacob and promised him and his seed the land he was living in at the time. **Genesis 28:12-13.** Then, we see where God got Moses' attention, through a burning bush, there was much dialog between the two of them—almost the entire third chapter of Exodus. **Exodus 3:4-22.** God speaks to children, too. For example, Samuel was a child when he had his first encounter with God. I don't have scripture for this, but I'd like to think Samuel was about the age of four. His young age probably contributed to his not being able to recognize the voice of God at first. God called him several times before his master Eli understood that it was the call of God, and instructed Samuel how to answer God. **I Samuel 3:1-14.** David, the second king of Israel, spoke with God also. During his kingship, he would inquire of God whether or not they were to go in battle. God would answer, "Yes go and you will be successful or don't go." **II Samuel 5:19.** The point is, God is yet speaking to His people through His written Word and into our spirit. We just need to listen and obey.

In the New Testament, at the beginning of the two of the four gospels (Matthew and Luke), the pattern of God speaking to his people seems to be through angels, visions and dreams, whereas in the Old Testament it was more directly to the individual/s. In all four books— Matthew, Mark, Luke and John—Jesus was here on earth with his twelve (12) disciples. Therefore, God's Word was with them; there wasn't a need for God to speak from heaven because they had heaven's best in the flesh. For example, in the New Testament, before the ministry of Jesus began. **Matthew 1:18-25**, an angel spoke to Joseph in a dream concerning the conception of Jesus, his birth and deity. Later in **Matthew 2:19**, an angel appeared to Joseph in another dream and summoned him to take Jesus and Mary to Israel for their safety. Baby Jesus' life was in danger of the murderer King Herod until his death. Then in **Luke 1:13**, an angel spoke to Zacharias and announced the birth of John the Baptist. Later in that same chapter **verses 27-38**, an angel sent from God spoke to Mary and said, "Listen, you are a blessed woman, you have been chosen by God, to bring the Savior into the world." Read and you will find that Gabriel (an angel) and Mary had a lengthy conversation. In **Acts 9:4**, Jesus had an encounter with Saul, who was on his way to Damascus to persecute more saints. Saul heard the voice of Jesus asking why he was being persecuting by him. Saul asked who you are. Jesus identified himself to Saul. It seems that they knew who God was in the Old Testament, but they had difficulty in recognizing his voice in the New Testament, so it was questioned as to who he was. Not only then, but today, it is yet the same question as to who Jesus is. John declares that Jesus was in the world, the world that he himself (Jesus) made, and the world didn't even recognize who he was. Are we yet in the blind today as to who Jesus is? **John 1:10.** This portion of scriptures has two main factors that jumps right up into our face. One, Jesus was in the physical world we now live in; and two, Jesus is identified as being here from the beginning, meaning the six days when God created the heavens and earth; not to mention when He said, "Let US make man," **Genesis 1:26.** Then **John 20:31** states that these scriptures are written specifically for our belief that Jesus Christ is the Son of the true and living God, as well as our eternal life with Him, when He returns to take us back with him.

Deuteronomy 4:9-10 says "Take heed to thyself, and keep thy soul diligently, lest thou forget the things which your eyes have seen, and lest they depart from thy heart all the days of thy life; but teach them to thy sons, and thy son's sons; The Lord said unto me, gather me the people together, and I WILL MAKE THEM HEAR MY WORDS, that they may learn to fear me all the days that they shall live upon the earth, and that they teach their children." Hearing God's Word is important, letting it dwell in us is more important according to **Colossians 3:16.** We must treasure the Word of God and ponder it in our hearts. The heart keeps the blood flowing. It is the vital part of life. Jesus is God's Word, in His Word, we have life, eternal and abundant life. Jesus is the vital part of our spiritual life that flows through us.

In Deuteronomy 5:5, Moses declares that he stood between the people and God just to show them the Word of God, because they were so afraid they would be consumed by the fire. You might ask, what words? The answer is the "Ten Commandments." However, Jesus narrowed the Ten Commandments down to two. **Matthew 22:36-40.** We all have an idea of what the Ten Commandments are, but some of us might not know what the two are. Jesus Himself in the New Testament narrowed the ten to two, which are, "We must love our Lord which is God with all of our heart, soul and mind." The second is similar, "We must love our neighbors just like we love ourselves." Now that's a loaded one. Jesus said that all the other commandments of the law and prophets hang on these two. I believe Jesus is saying in this portion of scripture that if we love God with all of our heart, soul and mind, and love our neighbors as well as ourselves, that this love covers all Ten Commandments and laws. Because when we love with pure love, there is no ill worked. Not only that, but if we love others like we love ourselves, those of us that love ourselves will look out for each other and treat them with understanding, love, respect and kindness. We won't be so judgmental, nor will we be so quick to lash out at each other, but rather forgive.

We have learned how potent our words are through experiences, hearing words and through the Word of God in the Bible. Yet I hear some say that the word Father is no name and Son is no name, just titles, especially referring to scripture concerning the Baptism. Yes they are titles and they are also names that God Himself has declared. God gave Himself many names in the Old Testament. In **Exodus 3:13-15**, When God sent Moses to tell the children of Israel that He was going to deliver them, Moses wanted to know, "Who should I tell the people sent me? They are not going to take my word for it." God said to Moses, "Just tell them, I AM THAT I AM sent you." Moses was meek and humble and obeyed the voice of God and conveyed that, "I AM has sent me, the God of Israel, and your fathers, Abraham, Isaac, and Jacob, that's a lasting memorial throughout all history forever." **In Exodus 6:2**, God spoke to Moses and said this: "I appeared to Abraham in a dream and my name to him was JEHOVAH, God Almighty."

Now in the New Testament, the words Father and Son are revealed in **II John, verse 3**, stating that "Grace, mercy and peace from God the Father and from the Lord Jesus Christ, the Son of the Father in truth and love." If we want to be specific in using the names opposed to titles as some say, then we need to baptize in the name of God the Father and Jesus Christ the Son, so we don't leave out neither the Father nor the Son. Every Word that proceeds out of the mouth of God is pure and true declares **Proverbs 30:5.** Father and Son are both Holy Ghost-filled, important Words. God and Jesus are revealed throughout the Old and New Testament. God spoke in the New Testament and said this is my beloved Son, whom I am well pleased. **Matthew 3:17.** Jesus plainly tells us that, he didn't do things on his own, but under the auspices of his Father God. **John 5:30-31.** David recognized Father and Son as Lord and Lord in **Psalms 110:1**, saying, "The Lord said to my Lord, sit thou on my right hand, until I make your enemies thy footstool." The grammatical part is such that it is plain to see David is referring to two, "Lord said to my Lord." Yes, Jesus is sitting on the right hand of His Father, our Father, Omnipotent, Wonderful, God Almighty, Counselor, all power, merciful God, Jesus Christ our redeemer, intercessor and everlasting savior.

People, we must study the Word of God, it is of utmost importance. If you don't, you will definitely have a lack of knowledge and a degree of ignorance. Why do I say that? Well, because I would be questioned as to why did I preach from the Old Testament? To be honest with one at that time, I wasn't prepared to give them good answers like I can now. The Old and New Testament relate and intertwine with each other. Not only that, but Jesus himself, during his ministry here on earth, often referred to both the Old and New Testaments. Jesus said he didn't come to destroy the Old Testament, but to fulfill it. You find prophetic prophecies throughout the Old Testament concerning Jesus. That is why I took the time to include so many scriptures from the Old Testament as well as the New. Sometimes the scriptures will overlap.

Jesus Christ is revealed in the New Testament as the Word of God. The Holy Ghost conceals the Word of God (the keeping power) within us in the New Testament also. Key points are, God sent His Son, our Lord and savior, the Holy Ghost our keeping power and Comforter. Jesus came down from heaven as a sacrificial offering from God (His Father) for our many sins, transgressions and redemption. **Isaiah 53:4.** Amen.

CHAPTER II

Jesus at Work before Creation

Genesis is the book of the beginnings. Genesis begins with progressive self-revelation of God that culminates in Christ. He has three primary names of Deity, Elohim, Jehovah, and Adonai. He has five important compound names found in Genesis. Genesis is throughout the New Testament, quoted approximately sixty times in seventeen books. Genesis inspiration and characters are a divine revelation, authenticated by the testimonies of the four gospels, **Matthew 19:4-6; 24:37-39; Mark 10:4-9; Luke 11:49-51; 17:26-29, 32; John 1:5; 7:21-23; 8:44, 56.**

Genesis gives us a glimpse or peek at Jesus; Isaiah paints a gigantic picture; and the New Testament tells the whole story. One might argue that God wasn't talking about Jesus in Genesis, but Jesus clarified it in the New Testament. He deeply expressed himself to his Father that he wanted to have that same intimate relationship and sweet commune that they had in the beginning, before the world was made. **John 17:5** seems to indicate this relationship the Father and Son had is precise and straight to the point. Look at the inferences He put on, calling on His Father, "Oh Father," he says. I believe Jesus remembered the closeness, with just the two of them together, before He came to this earth, and now that he had taken on this bitter task, just for us retched mortals called human beings, he felt lonely.

"Father" is the first person in the Trinity, according to the Webster Dictionary. **Psalms 89:26** declares that God is our Father, the rock of our salvation, and we are His children. **Isaiah 64:8** lets us know that not only is He our Father, but the potter that molds us—we—the clay into shape.

Remember three things, God can't lie, God can't die and God can't sin.

In Genesis God said, "Let US make man in OUR image, after OUR likeness; and let man have dominion over the fish in the sea, the fowl in the air, the cattle, the earth, and over every creeping thing that creep upon the earth. God created man in His own image, both male and female." **Genesis 1:26** notes that God spoke and everything came into being. But when it came to mankind, He made it known that it was more than one, with words such as US and OUR, words that denote plural, meaning more than one.

Man cannot make nor duplicate anything that's living, especially human beings. He is unable to catch air and hold it in his hands; neither can he restore the life of one, once life is gone. He has no control over the sun, moon nor stars. Everything God made is perfect. We are wonderfully and fearfully made by God. We are the ones who are destructive. We destroy our bodies with drugs, strong drinks, nicotine and promiscuous sex, and all kind of diabolical things.

Think about the sun, moon, galaxy and the sky which man cannot tamper. Now the astronauts proclaimed that they visited the moon. What happened after that? We began to have strange weather and polluted air. Just think for a moment: The sun and moon are billions of years old and never have had need of repair. What if they did? Our minds are just too small to conceive the works and wonders of God. God is Almighty and powerful, so much that we can't look at Him and live. The children of Israel couldn't stand the sound of His voice. We find another powerful verse in **Genesis 3:22.** "Look, man has become as one of US, to know the difference between good and evil." Who is the US? The Father, Son and the Holy Ghost, that's the US. We also find the third part of the trinity, the Holy Spirit, in the Old Testament as well. **Psalms 51:11** says "Cast me not away from thy presence; and take not thy Holy Spirit from me."

In the book of Genesis, God spoke and everything came into being. We also find in the Bible the power of our words. **Romans 4:17** tells us that we can call things that don't exist into existence. If that amount of power lies within our tongues, how much more, and greater God's Word is, when He speaks! When the apostles spoke and commanded the man to take up his bed and walk, faith through obedience moved into action, and action through hearing the Word of God, the man walked, leaped and ran according to **Acts 3:6.** I tell you words are powerful. My Bible tells me that the power of both death and life are in the power of our tongue, found in **Proverbs 18:21.** This tells me that we set our own stage of performance in life. That's why we must be careful of what we speak, because it will come into being. Therefore we must know that God's Word is even more powerful. We can depend on God's Word and His promise. According to the Word, we are saved through hearing the Word—the Word of God. The Word of God gives us power to overcome any and everything. If we operate in God's Word, we will grow both naturally and spiritually. Paul said in **Romans 10:8** that what's in our heart comes out in words. Then **Psalms 119:11** lets us know that he hid the Word in his heart so he wouldn't sin against God. When the Word is hid in our heart, it speaks to us. Now it's up to us to listen and obey. But sometimes, we override the Word and do what we want to do.

What a mighty voice in **Psalms 29:3-9.** It ripples the waters into the air moving with the wind, fierce and powerful in the thunder, up root trees, it can take a city and replace into another one, it can set flames of fire and spread it or divide it, yet full of majesty. The voice of God can turn a wilderness into a desert, can be heard through animals, make discoveries, raise the dead, give sight to the blind, command the flood and rain, stop the train, and the plane. It can move mountains, wipe out cities. The voice of Lord God will stop the battle, turn back the clock, He speak to the wind and it obey. The truth is, our words have power, and God intended for them to do so. Words can be more piercing than a stab or slap. People have spent many years in prison because of a lying tongue. On the other hand, prisoners have been released with one step forth with the truth. Words have caused nations to be destroyed. Words have strength—they can heal, damage, kill, destroy, save and they can cause one to be weak. Words bring happiness and sadness; they can encourage and discourage; they can build up and tear down; they can be used for instructions and destructions, build reputations, or they can be used as a witness for or against one. Words can curse or they can bless. God sent His Word via Jesus Christ for our salvation. Through Jesus Christ the Word of God, we are redeemed, through the shedding of His blood. The Word of God is mentioned approximately 161,000,000, in the Old Testament and approximately 179,000,000, in the New Testament.

The Bible contains the Word of God, it is not the Word of God. The word Bible is defined as a book of sacred writings, which is the Word of God.

Yes, our words are most important and powerful, both verbal and written. We make deals, commitments, agreements and oaths. We testify, write and trust in the words of others. Now we are made of dirt. God took dirt and made us. Then He breathed breath into us, gave us a spirit, body, and soul with a mind to think. Now God gave us the ability to do all what we do with ourselves, how much more powerful our creator is, than the creature. How it is that God would make us more powerful than Himself?

Here are a few things that can be done through the power of words, both natural and spiritual through Jesus Christ. We communicate our thoughts and feelings through our words. We make marital oaths, record history, we sanction, pray, sing, counsel, make and break promises, and deals. We can be healed through our faith and words. Jesus and the apostles spoke the Word and miracles were performed. Jesus opened the eyes of the blind, open the deaf ears, caused the lame to walk and dumb to talk. He even blessed two fishes and five loaves of bread with seven baskets left over, all with powerful words.

Sometimes our intellect is judged by our speech. We are the most intelligent species on the earth. We make our own decisions of what we are going to eat, wear, where we want to live, and work. Animals cannot convey their thoughts as humans do for their daily activities.

God gives directions. We give directions. God gives instructions, we give instructions. God gives warnings, we give warnings. God spoke the entire universe into existence and gave us the power as well to speak things into existence: **Romans 4:17.** He said we can speak to the mountain and cause it to move, not for us to walk around it, let alone strength to climb it. We don't need to use our strength to climb, when we have the power to speak the word and move it, hallelujah, amen. Once we realize the power that lies in our mouth, from the words which proceeds, we too will begin to see miraculous miracles happen. The power lies within our tongues: **Proverbs 18:21,** it's up to us to use it. My daily practice is to use it for my daily cleansing and healing.

God is a deliver, a healer, and He blesses. God detest complaining, grumbling, and mumbling. **I Chronicles** 10:13-14, Saul died because of his transgressions against the Word of the Lord, he failed to keep. He went to council with a witch instead of God. **I Chronicles 11:10,** David was made a king according to God's Word.

Chapter III

Who is Jesus in Isaiah?

Isaiah is a major prophet who predicted the coming and suffering of the Messiah. He received his prophetic ministry from God in a vision. Isaiah proclaimed that out of the lineage of David would come a Messiah who would establish His eternal rule among His people. Isaiah prophetic ministry was around 740 B.C. until approximately 701 B.C. Isaiah had more to say about the coming of our Lord and Savior in the Old Testament than all of the other prophets put together.

Prophecies Concerning Jesus' Lineage in Isaiah, Genesis And Jeremiah

The books of Genesis, Isaiah and Jeremiah cite Jesus as a righteous king that came through the lineage of Jessie and a branch of David to gather all of the nations and people, on the earth, to execute judgment for all **(Isaiah 11:1 and 10).**

We find in **Genesis 22:18**, when we listen and obey the voice of God, we will be blessed according to His Word. Blessings flow through great leaders that impart the Word of God into us, according to **Genesis 49:10.**

"Behold, the day come, said the Lord, that I will raise unto David a righteous Branch and a King shall reign and prosper, and shall execute judgment and justice in the earth." **(Jeremiah 23:5)**

Prophetic Character of Christ in Deuteronomy

God sent prophesy in the fifth book of the Pentateuch and foretold the coming of Christ. Not only that, but He let us know that Jesus would speak God's Words to us **Deuteronomy 18:15-19.** Whosoever listens and obey the Word of God will be blessed, and those that don't will be cursed.

Jesus Birth in Isaiah, Daniel and Micah

The Old Testament reveals the conception, birth, and suffering of Jesus Christ in **Isaiah 7:14-16. Isaiah 9:6-7** lets us know that with Jesus there is peace, and he would carry the weight of this old world on his shoulder.

Isaiah 48:16 spoke boldly. He was overt, with authority of speech. He didn't do it in a closet, nor did he bite his tongue, but proclaimed to the world, in the wide open, concerning the coming of Jesus Christ, the Son of God **Isaiah 50:5. Isaiah 62:11** let us know further, that not only was he entering this sinful world, but would bring salvation with him for us.

Daniel reads, "Know therefore and understand, that from the going forth of the commandment to restore and to build Jerusalem, unto the Messiah the Prince, shall be seven weeks, and three score and two weeks; the street shall be built again, and the wall, even in troublous times." **Daniel 9:25.**

Micah declares, "But thou Bethlehem Ephratah, though thy be little among the thousands of Judah, yet out of thee shall he come forth unto me that is to be the ruler in Israel: whose goings forth have been from of old, from everlasting. Therefore will he give them up, until the time that she which travails has brought forth: then the remnant of his brethren shall return to the children of Israel." **(Micah 5:2-3)** "And the redeemer shall come to Zion, and unto them which turn from transgression in Jacob, said the Lord." **(Isaiah 59:20)**

Jesus' Forerunner in Isaiah

There's no prophet like Isaiah. He foretold the forerunner of Jesus. John, who was his cousin, spoke the same words found in the New Testament as it is in Isaiah. "Prepare the way for the Lord, for he will make every crocked path straight." **Isaiah 40:5.**

Jesus Christ' Triumphal Entry in Psalms, Daniel, Zechariah and Philippians

"Blessed be he that comes in the name of the Lord." **Psalms 118:26.** "Then I lifted up mine eyes, and looked, and behold a certain man clothed in linen, whose loins were girded with fine gold of Uphaz: His body also was like the beryl, and his face as the appearance of lightning, and his eyes as lamps of fire, and his arms and feet like polished brass, and the voice of his words like the voice of a multitude." **Daniel 10:5-6.**

"Rejoice greatly, O daughter of Zion; shout, O daughter of Jerusalem: behold, thy king come unto thee; he is just, and having salvation; lowly, and riding upon an ass, and upon a colt the foal of an ass Zechariah." **Zechariah 9:9.**

Prophecies of Christ Appearance in the Temple in Haggai, and Malachi

"For thus said the Lord of host; yet once it is a little while, and I will shake the heavens, and the earth, and the sea, and the dry land; and I will shake all nations, and the desire of all nations shall come: and I will fill this house with glory, said the Lord of hosts.

"The glory of this latter house shall be greater than the former, said the Lord of host: and in this place will I give peace, said the Lord of hosts." **Haggai 2:6-7, 9.**

"Behold, I will send my messenger, and he shall prepare the way before me: and the Lord, whom ye seek, shall suddenly come to his temple, even the messenger of the covenant, whom ye delight in: behold, he shall come, said the Lord of hosts." **Malachi 3:1.**

Prophecies Concerning Jesus Preaching in Isaiah and Psalms

Isaiah continues with prophecies of Christ's being anointed to preach the gospel, bringing good tidings to the poor, mending broken hearts, comforting the meek and bringing freedom to those who are bound in sin, captivated by iniquity and burdened down with heavy hearts. Isaiah let us know that Jesus will bring peace, joy and happiness. In doing this, God will be glorified with the restoration of his children, through the righteousness of His Son Jesus Christ. **Isaiah 61:1-3 and Isiah 11:2-5.**

This is the way **Psalms 40:9-10** put it: Righteousness has been preached to the vast congregation. I didn't hold anything back. I told them everything God conveyed to me. I was gracious, I did it with love, so it would be accepted by them.

Miracles of Christ Jesus in Isaiah

These are some of the miracles of Jesus performed that Isaiah foretold. The Prophet Isaiah was so clear and precise, how could one suggest that the Old Testament should not be included in the sermons of today. How could they not clearly see all the prophecies, fulfilled in the New Testament, that were prophesied in the Old Testament? The New Testament fulfills the Old—Jesus healing blind eyes, unstopping deaf ears and making the crocked path straight. This is twofold, meaning first natural, then spiritual. **Isaiah 29:18.**

A few chapters later, Isaiah goes on to tell us that our eyes won't become dim, and neither will our ears become hard of hearing. The stutters will have clear speech and the dumb will sing hallelujah. **Isaiah 32:3-4** and **Isaiah 35:5-6.**

What a glorious time that will be; nothing like we've ever seen before. Everything will be perfect, righteous and there will be continuous joy, peace and happiness. We'll never be forgotten nor taken for granted. Jesus took all the suffering of lashings, being spat on and having pulling out patches of His hair pulled out, that Isaiah prophesied, just so we could be heirs with Him and the Father. **Isaiah 42:15-16.**

Jesus' Suffering, Scourging and Contempt in Isaiah and Silence at his Trial

When we think of suffering, usually it's not the kind of suffering Jesus went through. Isaiah deemed that Jesus was bound to suffer for all of our transgressions, sins and all iniquities. Not only did He go through it, but it wasn't for something He did, but for what we did. I often try to figure out, why we can't endure small sufferings, such as people lying on us, misusing us, or mistreating us, sometimes after we've been their lifeline. I know it hurt, but just think, Jesus was destined to do good ONLY, and He also was destined to suffer cruel treatment. In spite of all the good He did, He suffered beatings until His skin ripped off of His body, and had thorns put on His head for a crown. Now, if Jesus went through such agony, pain and suffering out of all the good He did, for the bad we did, why can't we endure a small bit of ill treatment? Why can't we be obedient? Why can't we love each other? Why can't we forgive each other? Why can't we do well to our neighbors? Why? Why? What more can He do? He laid the foundation and opened up the way. What more can He do? God loved us so much that He gave his only begotten Son. Why? For our right to the tree of life, to live with the Father, forever and ever.

At one point Isaiah wanted to know who would believe the report of Jesus' coming, the savior and Son of God? People, we are yet in doubt that Jesus Christ is the Son of God, in spite of all the good that He did, and sufferings he went through. They rejected Him then, and refuse to recognize Him now as the savior. Yet, out of all the unbearable punishment he endured, for our iniquities, what did He do? Poured out his soul, knowing He was on his way to be crucified like a sinner, and NEVER complained "Why me, what did I do to deserve this?" Yes, just for us and our wicked ways, so that we have this undeserved right to the kingdom. **Isaiah 50:5-6** and **Isaiah 53:1-12.**

Jesus Christ's Betrayal and the Apprehension (Agreement of Judas to Betray Christ)

Prophecies Applied To Judas in Psalms and Zechariah

The people I put trust in, the people I feed, the people I healed, the people I restored their health and life, the people I nurtured, and counseled, those are the ones that turned their backs on me, threw me under the bus, rolled over me both ways to make sure I was dead. I became worthless to them, so they sold me for a few pieces of silver. **Psalms 69:25, Psalms 109:8 and Zachariah 11:12-13.**

Prophecies of Jesus Christ between the Two Thieves in Isaiah and Insults in Psalms

The prophecies of Jesus Christ hanging between the two thieves was foreseen in Isaiah. Everything that would happen to Jesus, His insults, death, parting of His garment, his silence and his accusations were all recorded in the book of **Isaiah 53:1-12.**

Not only did they throw insults at Him, but they heckled Him, laughed at Him, poked fun and jeered Him. Ok, you claim to be the Son of God, let's see Him help you now! **Psalms 22:8** and **18.** They gave him vinegar instead of water, and bitter gall to eat. **Psalms 69:21.**

I want you to use your imagination. You are thirsty on death row, you ask for water, and are given vinegar. You are guilt free. You did only good and righteousness. They can't find anything that you did, but the public wants you dead—the same people you helped, the same people that worshipped you just yesterday. Now those same people want you dead, in spite of your suffering for our cause, sins and for the iniquities of the whole world. **Psalms 109:25.**

Christ's Death Recorded in Numbers, Psalms, Isaiah and Daniel

The description of Jesus' death, in the Old Testament, leaves one to believe and know that the stage was set before the world began. Our God knew that we would sin and need His Son to be a sacrificial offering for the redemption of our salvation. Therefore it was predestined He would live a short period of time in this physical world. He would be crucified, with no bones broken, his burial would be among the transgressors and sinners. **Numbers 9:12 and Psalms 22:14-16.**

He was taken from prison and from judgment—and who shall declare his generation? He was cut out of the land of the living. For the transgression of my people was he stricken? And He made his grave with the wicked, and with the rich in his death; because He had done no violence, neither was any deceit in his mouth. **Isaiah 53:8-9.**

"Who is this that comes from Edom, with dyed garments from Bozrah? This that is glorious in his apparel, traveling in the greatness of his strength? I that speak in righteousness, mighty to save." **Isaiah 63:1.**

Prophecies of Christ's Resurrection in Psalms

I have set the Lord always before me because he is at my right hand. I shall not be moved. Therefore my heart is glad, and my glory rejoice: my flesh also shall rest in hope. For thy will not leave my soul in hell; neither will thou suffer thine Holy One to see corruption **Psalms 16:8-10.**

Christ Ascension in Psalms

You have ascended on high, you have led captivity captive: thou has received gifts for men; yea, for the rebellious also, that the Lord God might dwell among them **Psalms 68:18.**

CHAPTER IV

—ɯ—

Miscellaneous Prophecies in the Old Testament

There are so many prophecies concerning Jesus in the Old Testament, therefore I will just list their headings and scriptures where they are found.

Opposition of Rulers: Psalms 2:1-3
Christ's Humanity: Genesis 3:15
Psalms 22:22 - Isaiah 8:18
Christ Divinity: Psalms 2:7 and 12
Psalms 45:6-7 - Psalms 72:15 and 17
Isaiah 9:6 - Jeremiah 23:6
Zeal: Psalms 69:9 - Isaiah 59:16-19
Jesus Christ Meekness: Isaiah 42: 2-3
Justification: Isaiah 42:21 - Jeremiah 33:16
Daniel 9:24
Sacrifice Psalms: 40:6-8 - Isaiah 53:4-6, 10-11
Christ's Priesthood: I Samuel 2:35 - Psalms 110:4
Christ's Kingship: Psalms 2:6 – Psalms 45:1, 3-5
Psalms 110:1-2, 5-6 - Isaiah 9:7
Prophecies in the Old Testament continued:
Isaiah 16:5 - Isaiah 22:20-22 - Isaiah 32:1-2
Isaiah 55:3-4 - Jeremiah 30:9 - Ezekiel 37:24-25
Daniel 7:13-14 – Hosea 3:5 – Haggai 2:23
Jesus Christ as Shepherd: Ezekiel 34:23 –
Micah 5:4-5 – Zechariah 13:7
Christ as the Lamb: Isaiah 53:7 – John 1:29
Acts 8:32-35 – I Peter 1:19 – Revelation 5:6

Remember three things, God can't lie, God can't die and God can't sin.

Christ as the Branch: Isaiah 4:2
Jeremiah 33:14-15 – Ezekiel 17:22-24
Ezekiel 34:29 - Zechariah 3:8 - Zechariah 6:12-13
Christ as the Fountain: Zechariah 13:1
Christ as the Sword: Isaiah 49:1-4
Christ the Corner-Stone: Psalms 118:22-24
Isaiah 28:16 - Zechariah 3:9
Christ as a Stumbling-Stone: Isaiah 8:14-15
Christ as a Light: Isaiah 42:6-6
Christ as the Sun: Malachi 4:2
Christ as the Star: Numbers 24:17
Christ's Relations with Herod: Jeremiah 31:15-17

IS JESUS GOD?
IN THE
NEW TESTAMENT

CHAPTER V

—*m*—

Jesus Christ the Word of God

The New Testament consists of actual scriptures with definite statements relating to our God and His Son Jesus Christ. Jesus as the Word, proceeding out of the mouth of God in Genesis, and Jesus as the Word of God made flesh in Matthew through Revelations. Thus revealing the Father and the Son in full knowledge, from the beginning (Genesis) to the end (Revelation). Words are close to us, whether we want them to be or not. They are in our heart, mouth, thoughts and all languages. Therefore, we should study the Word of God so the right kind of Word will be in us, propelling us to obey. **Deuteronomy 30:14.** Paul repeats these exact words in **Romans 10:8**, in the New Testament.

Words are infinity. You can repeat the same word trillions of times and it will never fade, nor will it become obsolete. Words do not fade or faint. As long as you live, you can say the same words over and over again. Words are thoughts brought into focus. You can think of what you are going to say and decide whether or not you are going to say it. Words are powerful in a negative and/or positive way. Words with the same meaning can be spoken and understood in many different languages. Words are dark and colorful. Words take on spirits in which they are sent, said or thought.

Sad to say we haven't learned how to capitalize on the power of our words in a more positive way. Example: The scriptures tell us to speak to the mountain to be moved from one place to another, believing that it will be done. **Matthew 17:20.** I am so amazed at the things that God does, through my thoughts, faith or just mere asking. He turns things around from a negative to a positive. I can refer back to the scripture where Joseph told his brothers, "You thought evil against me, but God meant it for good." **Genesis 50:20.** God is eternal life.

We seem to be excellent at speaking negative thoughts instead of positive things that will benefit us. One portion of scripture tells us that death and life are in the power of our tongue. Most of us speak death as opposed to life. Our tongue power should be to edify God. **Proverbs 18:21.**

Our words are within us wherever we go, in our thoughts, mind, in sleep during our dreams, and in our speech. When we communicate, our words go out and they are heard by ourselves and others. Guess what? God is so mighty and powerful, He allows us to copy and duplicate whatever He does. For example, He sent His Word in written form in the Bible, His Word Jesus Christ in the flesh, and the Holy Spirit. We can and do, send our words, both spoken, and written, through the flesh, telegraph, phone, thoughts and through our spirits. Wow! That is powerful. Our words can be in one place and we in another, even in different languages, books, papers, and magazines. Whatever we speak, it should be beneficial. As Paul put it, "Let what we speak be honest, pure, true, lovely, just and of a good report, that will increase our spirituality."

I like to think on things that will help me to grow more spiritual and fruitful in Christ Jesus. I ask God to help me improve my thought pattern and fulfill my purpose while I'm here on this side of the kingdom. Paul states that we should have the mind of Christ in us. What was that mind? Christ had a mind to be obedient to God, although he was in the form of God. He didn't get uplifted, like Lucifer. He never pointed at himself, but always directed the honor and glory to his Father, God. Jesus was humble; we too must be humble. When we are, God Himself will exalt us, just as He did for His Son, Jesus Christ. **Philippians 2:5-11.**

The four gospels address the living Word Jesus Christ as the Son of God while living here on earth. Acts reveal his purpose here after his death and resurrection.

Although all 26 books of the New Testament reveal Jesus Christ as the Son of God, John is the most profound. He indeed earned the accolades as John the beloved, for his prolific view of Jesus Christ.

Matthew, the first book in the New Testament, seems to direct most of his writings towards the Old Testament, which shows Jesus Christ as the Messiah, especially in Isaiah. Matthew's central theme stresses that Jesus Christ is the long-waited king of the Kingdom of God.

Jesus Christ was the Word of God born in the flesh, that we might have a right to the tree of life in the New Testament. In the Old Testament, our redeemer will come; in the New Testament, our redeemer is here, and we are redeemed through the blood of the lamb. Now we can say we have hid the Word of God in our heart, so we won't sin against Him. **Psalms 119.**

Jesus Christ Genealogy in Matthew and Luke

Matthew and Luke, two scribes out of the four gospel writers in the New Testament, reveal the genealogy of Jesus Christ. The book of **Matthew 1:1-17**, parallel with **Isaiah 11:1** and **10** concerning Jesus Christ's genealogy, shows that Jessie is the father of David the king, and David, the king father of Solomon. Jacob is the father of Joseph, Mary's husband, and Mary is Jesus' mother. Although Luke wrote the genealogy of Jesus Christ, it isn't as clear as that of Matthew. **Luke 3:23-38** genealogy records that Jesus, the supposed son of Joseph, was about thirty years old when he began his ministry. Joseph's father was Heli, the son of Matthat and so on through forty-two generations.

Prophecies concerning Christ's lineage in the Old Testament can be found in **Genesis 22:18, Genesis 49:10, Isaiah 11:10 and Jeremiah 7:23:5.**

The Birth of Jesus Christ in Isaiah, Matthew and Luke

It is believed that Mary, the mother of Jesus, was a peasant woman from the town of Nazareth, a city in Galilee, from the tribe of Judah, in the linage of David. An angel announced Jesus' birth in **Luke 1:32.** Mary was highly favored enough to give birth to the Son of God. Deriving from the scriptures, Mary was rich in character but low in material goods. She didn't have proper clothes for the child, neither did she have a proper place to give birth to Him. Matthew phrased it to say "Mary was found with child." Note the above in Luke, where Gabriel announced to her she was with child. In Matthew the angel spoke to Joseph, telling him that Mary was having a child, conceived of the Holy Ghost. **John 1:1** doesn't mention the birth of Jesus, however he tells us about his existence before he was born into the world in the flesh. "In the beginning was the Word, and the Word was with God, and the Word was God." The birth of Jesus in the Old Testament can be found in **Isaiah 7:14.** "Behold, a virgin shall conceive and bear a son, and shall call his name Immanuel." **Isaiah 9:6-7** states, "Unto us a child is born, unto a son is given."

Christ's Forerunner (John) in Isaiah, Matthew, Mark, Luke and John

John was the forerunner of Jesus as a preacher, his morals, ministry, message and even his death. John is in all four gospels harmoniously. He also preceded Jesus in discipleship. John the Baptist was the first cousin of Jesus. His baptism practices served as a symbolic moral reform by *repenting* and *baptizing.* John the Baptist was mentioned as the forerunner of Jesus Christ in the Old Testament **Isaiah 40:3-5,** and in the New Testament in **Matthew 3:3-4, Mark 1:2-3, Luke 3:4 and John 1:23.**

The Revelation of who Jesus is in the Announcement of His Birth

Who Jesus is was established long before His entering this physical world in the natural, according to Moses, the great Prophet Isaiah and others.

Brother Luke brings into focus of who Jesus is through the conception of the Holy Ghost, and a bit of genealogy. *Mary, you are going to have a male child. I want you to name him Jesus. He is going to be great and rule the house of Jacob forever with no end to his kingdom.* How many of us can question GOD, as she did? She retorted, "How is that? I haven't slept with a man." Little did she know the Holy Ghost had taken over her body with no human involvement. With God, nothing is impossible. She birthed the Son of the True and Living God, for our many sins. Mary, a human, had a supernatural experience through God. **Luke 1:30-35 and 37.**

Chapter VI

—⁓⁓—

Who Am I in Baptism? Matthew, Mark and Luke

The conversation shown below between Jesus and God, defining who Jesus is, clearly distinguishes that there are two conversing in two different locations—Jesus on earth and God in heaven. First is God speaking in reference to His Son: "Now when all the people were baptized, and praying, the heaven was opened, and the Holy Ghost descended in a bodily shape like a dove upon Him (good God), AND A VOICE CAME FROM HEAVEN, which said (paraphrased), YOU ARE MY BELOVED SON; IN YOU I AM WELL PLEASED." **Luke 3:21-22.** This portion of scripture denotes the recognition of Jesus as being the Son of God.

Next, Brother Luke records that Jesus prayed to His Father all night. Can you explain to me how God prayed to Himself, or even why? No, Jesus the Word of God prayed to God His Father. We must realize that the Word emanates from God just as the Holy Ghost does. That is why we must strive to study God's Word, so it becomes a part of us, inside of us, even in our heart. **Luke 6:12.**

"Who Am I?" must be a very significant part of the scriptures. Why? Because Jesus asked His disciples in the midst of His praying, what are the people saying about me, whom do they think I am? John the Baptist answered, some say you are Elias, and some think that you are one of the old prophets that came back. Jesus asked a second time, but this time he directed His question to His disciples, "Who do you say I am?" Peter answered him immediately, "You are the Christ of God." Note, Peter said the Christ of God, meaning Jesus is a part of God. **Luke 9:18.**

Remember three things, God can't lie, God can't die and God can't sin.

Later, in **Luke 9:28-33**, Jesus is transfigured. During His Transfiguration, Moses and Elias appeared. Peter gets all excited and speaks all out of terms. During his excitement and speaking out of terms, a cloud appeared and covered them, and a voice came from the clouds and declared **(verse 35)**, "This is my beloved Son, hear Him." God repeatedly states that Jesus is His Son. Now if God physically came down Himself, wouldn't He say it? God is God all by Himself. He can do all things, but He can't lie! Another favorable scripture that put a difference between Jesus the Son of God and God the Father is **John 3:16**, for God so loved the world that He gave His only begotten Son, that whosoever believeth (continually) in him should not perish, but have everlasting life. **Matthew 3:17.**

Where Jesus was Before Entering the Earth in John

In the beginning, God's Word was with Him. Are not our words with us? And the Word was, and yet is, the Word of God. God never changed— His Word is yet with Him, according to the scriptures, sitting on His right hand. Jesus is that Word. All God did was spoke His Word, and everything fell into place. Wouldn't it be wonderful if everything we spoke positive would fall into place, just like that—or even greater, if we had enough light to eradicate the sin out of people? Jesus Christ can, because he is the light of the world. But He won't force Himself on us. It's a, "Whosoever will, let them come." Jesus said as many of us who receive him, and to those that believe on his name, he will give them that power to become the sons of* God. We don't have the power that God has. Of course not. But we are good copycats. Now we have voice mail, email, Western Union and all kinds of modern technology. We are limited only to what God will allow us to do. **John 1:1-17.**

notice the little two letter word "of." It is powerful and has a great significance in its meaning and use in the context. Examples: of God, of whom, of the Holy Ghost, and not of this world etc. meaning out from, originated, out of, the latter not from.

Jesus purpose for Coming in Mark/ Recognized by Demons

In Mark, Jesus is seen as the mighty worker who came to minister, a Servant-Son, and an emancipator. Demons recognized who Jesus was and why he came. They tried to discourage him from attacking them, by yelling, "Leave us alone. What do we have to do with you, you Jesus of Nazareth? Did you come to destroy us? I know you, you are the Holy one of God." **Mark 1:23-2.** Jesus' purpose was and is to destroy the devil and all his demonic work. As soon as we come to that realization, we will be able to live in a closer relationship with God through His Son Jesus Christ.

CHAPTER VII

Jesus as the Son According to John

John is the fourth writer of the gospel of Jesus Christ. His main purpose was set forth to identify who Jesus Christ is. **John 1:1-14**, reveals the Christ deity, Jesus as the light and His incarnation.

Has anyone ever seen God? No, not according to **John 1:18**. No one has ever seen God at any time. Only His begotten Son, who is in the bosom of the Father, has seen him." God can't lie, neither can he die. We must realize that Jesus Christ emanates from God. He is out from God. He is the Word of God. God's Word has life. That is the eternal life we are striving for.

Jesus Declares God Sent Him and is his Teacher and Father

Jesus Christ takes no credit for any work that He does, as we do so often. We pray and have faith. Someone gets healed and we take the credit; someone gets saved and we feel we are responsible. Jesus Christ didn't do that. He gives all the credit to His Father God. We must do the same—give the credit to God and stop shining the light on ourselves.

The Jews were so upset over Jesus healing the impotent man on the Sabbath, and being equal with God, that they sought to kill Him. Nowadays, merchants' largest days of sales are on our day we set aside for our Sabbath (Sundays). I recall when that wasn't true. All stores were closed on Sundays. Not only that, I find people doing their household chores, playing sports, going to the beach, shopping and all kind of things on Sundays, the day we set aside as our Sabbath. Again, after their accusations, Jesus yet gives His Father God all honor and credit.

Jesus said, "I need for you to understand, I can't do anything by myself. But, whatever things I see my Father do, I do them as well." Because of the love the Father has for me, He shows me all of His great works, like raising the dead, giving sight to the blind and making the lame walk and the dumb talk. **John 5:19.** My Father doesn't judge either, but has committed all judgments to me. Therefore we all should honor Jesus, as we honor God, who sent Him. **John 5:20.**

Jesus healed on the Sabbath, which caused a great uproar among the Jews. They claimed that it was unlawful, according to Moses law. Jesus let them know He was doing the work of his Father. This caused them to be even angrier at Him, enough to take his life, calling God His Father, making Himself equal with God. **John 5:7-18.**

In the Old Testament, Moses and the prophets heard the voice of God. Now, in the New Testament, the voice of God is through Jesus, His Son. Note that God admonishes us to hear the voice of His Son throughout the New Testament. "This is my beloved Son hear ye him." **Luke 9:35.** Hear what He has to say, for in what Jesus Christ speaks, are eternal Words, Words of eternal life. Jesus acknowledges God as His Father and that His *Father sent him* in almost every sentence—certainly in the four Gospels—repeatedly. It seems to me that Jesus wants us to know that God sent Him. He didn't decide to come; he obediently came. Jesus said in **John 12:28,** "**Father I want you to glorify your name.**" *God spoke from heaven answering Him.* "**I have glorified both of US, and will glorify it** again." **Hebrew 1:5.** *"You are my Son, this day have I begotten you."* God said, "**I will be to him a Father, and he shall be to me a Son.**" **II Peter 1:17.** Jesus received from God the Father, the excellent glory—honor and glory. *God let us know that,* "**This is my beloved Son, in whom I am well pleased.**"

In **John 5:24,** We that **hear** Jesus' Word, and **believes** that God **sent Him**, will have everlasting life, and will not be subjected to condemnation; but will be passed from death to life, in that great resurrection day. The life that God has given to Jesus, Jesus has given to us as heirs of God—His father. But those of us who don't believe won't share any part with Him. **John 5:47 and John 8:25-42.**

In **John 8:42-43,** Jesus came out from God, not from himself, but God send Him out from Him. Therefore, Jesus questions what it is that we don't understand. Is it his speech, or are we deaf and unable to hear?

It didn't matter how much Jesus told them He was sent by His Father, nor did it matter how many miracles He wrought, they became worse. They accused him of being a Samaritan and demon-possessed. Jesus retorted, "I don't have a devil. I honor my Father and you dishonor me." The Jews said, "Now we know for real that you are. Your father is the devil and no truth in him."

In **John 9:1-40, in** spite of all their denial of Jesus being the Son of God, Jesus continued to perform miracles. He healed the blind man's eyes. You would think He did a good deed that would be appreciated. Not according to the Pharisees and Jews. They contend that they were aware of God speaking to Moses, but they had problems with what Jesus proclaimed, saying He was from God and God is His Father, and that He received all of His instructions from God. Where did this Jesus come from? They continued to criticize and see evil in all He did. They needed a valid reason to kill Him, but kept running into a brick wall. They questioned the blind man's parents concerning his healing. However, the parents were reluctant to answer them; instead they referred them to their son for answers. The disciples wanted to know who sinned, the blind man or his parents. Jesus let them know that this was a part of the work that His Father sent him to do, not that anyone had committed sin. But, He had to work while it's day, signifying we need to do the work of God now, while we yet have life in our natural physical bodies, because we cannot work after we are dead. The rich man and poor man gave us a vivid picture of that. **Luke 16:19.** Now, Jesus never stopped working. He worked on the cross, in the grave and during and after the resurrection. Jesus worked while He was on earth, because He is the light of the world, then, now and forever.

Ten Declarations of Jesus Christ's Union with His Father

1. The Son can do nothing of Himself (**John 5:17, 19; 8:18**)
2. I of my own self do nothing (**John 5:30**)
3. I seek not mine own will, but the will of the Father (**John 5:30; 6:38**)
4. My doctrine is not mine, but His that sent Me (**John 7:16; 8:26, 38**)
5. I do nothing of Myself (**John 8:28**)
6. I do always those things that please Him (**John 8:29**)
7. I came from God, neither came I, neither came I of myself (**John 8:42; 16:28**)
8. I seek not mine own glory (**John 8:50, 54**)
9. I have not spoken of Myself, but the Father gave Me commandment what to speak (**John 12:49-50; 14:10**)
10. My works are not Mine, but the Father doeth the works (**John 10:25, 37-38; 14:10-11**)

Jesus reveals the union between him and His Father. Through that union, came obedience to His Father. That obedience was in His wiliness to lay down his life as a sacrificial offering for His sheep and their transgressions. Because of His obedience came the abundance of love from the Father to the Son.

I'm sure God and Jesus had conversations concerning this from the beginning. They already had a plan made for us. He showed power— "He" being the Son of God—to both lay down his life and take again. The most important thing is that this is a commandment he received from his Father God. **John 10:15-18.**

CHAPTER VIII

Jesus and His Father (God) at Work

In the scriptures you'll find phrases like, "You know Him, you know me, and you've seen me, you've seen Him." These are general statements I often used concerning my mother and I. Sometimes we were mistakenly misidentified. Jesus used such phrases, referring to the attributes of His being physically separated and spiritually united with His Father. The following statements exemplify the unity of Father and Son working together to get the job done. What I see my Father do, I do. What are some of the things Jesus did? He opened the blind eyes, made the lame to walk, the dumb to talk, raised the dead to life, turned water into wine, etc.

These are some of the works Jesus did: He performed surgery on the man's ear Peter amputated, fed multitudes at a time with a few pieces of fish and bread crumbs, according to the crowd they had. Jesus set up shop with a fish market and bakery, multiplied the crumbs into loaves of bread and two fishes into large portions, enough to feed five thousand people, with baskets full of left overs.

John 10:25-30: Please note that Jesus never gave credit to Himself. How many of us can say that? I listened to a healing ministry on television the other day, and with every other word, he was praising himself. What happen when I prayed for you? That word "I" is going to get a lot of us into trouble. I find that giving God the credit is seemingly an afterthought, from what I've observed. We are sheep, followers of Christ, we listen to his voice and obey it. God does not share His glory with anyone. So why are we trying to shine light on ourselves? I'm the great healer, great prophet and great orator? No, God is, He speaks to us and through us, He is the healer, not us.

John 10: 32, 34-38: Jesus said that his Father shows him many good things, and he likewise passes it on down to us. God said it, and I believe it. I've had many experiences with God. I know without a shadow of a doubt that God works through people and perform miracles. When you walk, talk and obey God, He does things that only He could do. Nothing is impossible with God. He opens doors that no man can shut and shut doors that no man can open.

John 11:4, 41-42: Jesus lifted up His eyes, and said, *"Father, I thank you for hearing me. I know that you hear me. You always listen to what I have to say. But because of the people that's near me, I want them to believe as well, that you sent me into this world."*

John 13:1, 3, 31-32: Jesus knew that His time was up doing the work here on this earth and that it was time for Him to return to His Father, in heaven. So He prepared the last supper with Himself and His twelve disciples. They broke bread and had wine for the last time together to commemorate His suffering on Calvary. Again, He did it just for us rank sinners. This did not take away the love Jesus had for them, although He knew he was going to be betrayed by Brother Judas.

"Listen I need for you to believe me that I am in the Father, and the Father in me: if you have problems believing, look at it for the work's sake. If you would just believe me, you will be able to do the same and greater work. Guess, what? I'll be right there for you, as long as you ask it in my name, you got it. Because my Father loves to glorify me, therefore it will be granted to you" **John 14:23-25, 28-31.** "Now if you do these things, showing your love for me, by listening and not only listening but abiding by my words, you will live with me in my Father's house. Remember, they are not my Words, but my Father's, the one that sent me Jehovah God." **John 15:1-5.** We are cleansed through the Word of God, therefore it behooves us to indulge in it daily. Just like taking our bath daily, we need a daily spiritual cleansing through God's Word, better known as the words contained in the Bible. In other words get in the Word and let the Word get in you. **John 15:1-5.**

Jesus Doing the Will of the Father/John

Jesus warned his followers not to work towards natural goals, but spiritual, for it will give them everlasting life. They in turn wanted to know what work they had to do. Jesus said, "Just believe in me, and that my Father God sent me. Know that the manna given in the desert wasn't given by Moses, but by my Father. Now He has given me to you, the true bread from heaven. Through me, you will never hunger nor thirst again, because in me is the true light for the entire world." Now, they wanted the bread non-stop! Jesus said, "Just believe that I am that bread and it will be forever flowing without stopping. But you first must believe. I continue to tell you who I am, showing you who I am, doing the work of who I am, and you are yet in doubt. You don't believe me. All that the Father gives me shall come to me; and him that comes to me I will in no wise cast out. *For I came down from heaven, not to do mine own will, but the will of Him that sent me. This is the Father's will which has sent me, that of all which he has given me I should lose nothing, but should raise you up again the last day. This is the will of Him that sent me, that everyone who sees the Son, and believes in Him, may have everlasting life: and I will rise Him up at the last day."* **John 6:27-40.** Jesus concludes in the **43 and 44ᵗʰ verses,** "Don't mumble and grumble with each other, because no one can get to the Father which has sent me, unless they are drawn by him and I will raise them up the last day. The prophets wrote they shall be taught of God. Every one that hears, and learns of the Father, comes to me. Not that anyone has seen the Father, only me, which is of God [there goes the 'of God' again), I have seen and do the will of my Father."

Jesus Reveals his Origin and Possessions

The following scriptures will show the unity of the Father and Son, as well as Jesus' origin.

John 16:15-16, 25-30: I'm speaking to you in parables now, but later, I will be more precise. I am getting ready to return to heaven and prepare it for you. So when I return, it will be to take you there. All things that the Father has are mine now.

A Perspective of Jesus through John

John doesn't waste any time. He starts out with a bang. "In the beginning was the Word, and the Word was *with God,* and the Word was *God.* This is where a lot of people get confused. Now it states that the Word was God. Yes the Word is God's Word, just like your words come from you when you speak. It is what you say. Therefore, we must be careful what we say or even think. The Rev. Dr. Martin Luther King Jr. is a prime example of it in his "I Have a Dream" speech. Although he didn't live to see that dream take place, it happened.

Jesus was with God in the beginning. Through Him all things were made; without Him nothing was made that has been made. In Him was life, and that life was the light of all people. **John 1:1-4. John 1:10 states,** "He was in the world and the world was made by Him and the world knew Him not." **John 1:12-14 states,** "But as many as received him, to them gave them power to become the sons of God, even to them that believe on his name. Which were born, not of blood, nor of the will of the flesh, nor of the will of man, but of God. And the Word was made flesh, and dwelt among us, (and we beheld his glory, the glory as of the only begotten of the Father,) full of grace and truth." Now listen to **John 1:18:** *"No man has seen God at any time; the only begotten Son, which is in the bosom of the Father, He has declared Him."* **John 5:19-23** reads like this: *"Verily, verily, I say unto you, the Son can do nothing of himself, but what he sees the Father do; for what things so ever he does, these also do the Son likewise. For the Father loves the Son, and shows him all things that himself do: and he will show him greater works than these, that you may marvel. For the Father raises up the dead, and quickens them; even so the Son quickens whom he will. For the Father judges no man, but has COMMITTED all judgment unto the Son: That all men should honor the Son, even as they honor the Father. He that honors not the Son, honors not the Father, which has sent him."*

My Bible tells me that God sent His Son Jesus. Now some say that God came down himself. Tell me how does that fit in? Some describe the Trinity as God, Jesus and the Holy Ghost or Holy Spirit as the three parts of an egg. We must remember that God is infinite. He said His Word is His Son. God did not leave heaven, enter the earth and die.

God cannot die, God cannot stand the sight of sin and God can't lie. What part of *sent* don't we understand? Had God came himself, the Bible would have said, "God came down." It stated that He came down in the Garden of Eden in the cool of the evening in Genesis and spoke to Adam, didn't He? It stated that He came down and spoke to Moses one-on-one, in Genesis, Exodus and Numbers, to give him instructions for the Israelites. God is Truth and not a lie.

Jesus Prays to His Father God/Preparing to Exit this World

John 17:1-3, 4-25: Jesus, the Word of God, continued to glorify God, as well as asking God the Father to glorify Him, according to the power He had been given.

Now let us take a careful note as Jesus prays. He prayed to His Father God, concerning Himself, Jesus the Son. Not only that but, He asked His Father to glorify Him (Jesus). Glorify according to Webster Dictionary is defined as "giving glory, honor, or high praise to; exalt." Jesus prays to Lord God, His Father, "Let them know you through me your Son. Glorify me, exalt me, lift me up, give me power, that as many will come to you, will come and know you through me as the one and only true God." Jesus concludes this portion of scripture by saying, "I have glorified thee on earth; I have finished the work which thou gave me to do." God glorified Him (Jesus) by saying, "This is my beloved Son, whom I am well pleased. Hear ye Him." Jesus went on to say, "I have manifest your name unto the men which you gave me out of the world: they were yours Father, and you gave them to me), and they have kept thy Word." That is the purpose of Jesus coming, so we would be able to keep the Word inside of us. One portion of scripture says "thy Word have I hid in my heart that I might not sin against thee." **Psalms 119:11.** The Word is truth, power, spirit and salvation. It keeps us, and set us free from sin. The Word is Jesus. *"Now they know that all things you have given me are of you. For I have given to them the Words which you gave me; and they have received them, and have known that I came out from you for sure, and they believe that you did send me. I pray for them: I pray for the world, but, the ones you gave me; they are mine; and now I'm glorified in them* (Jesus referring to His disciples), *I am prepared to leave them here, in this* *old world, I have confidence that they will be all right. Therefore Father I'm returning home to you.* This is Jesus making intercessory prayer for His disciples and future believers and making preparation to leave this old sinful world and to return to God, His Father.

The latter part of Jesus praying to His Father in John 17:13-26: Now Father, I'm coming to you; concerning those I'm leaving behind in this world. I want them to have joy, inner peace in abundance, and the Words that I speak, inside of them. I want them to be able to live sanctified and holy down here on this earth through truth, the way you planned it from the beginning. Father I'm not just praying for these alone, but I'm praying for all future generations and believers that will believe the report we have left behind. What should we believe? Believe the Word of God and that Jesus is that Word, and was sent to us from God His Father. Father, I want them to be with us in glory and see the kind of love you have for me, before the foundation of the world was laid.

Jesus continued to pray, "Oh righteous Father, the world didn't know you! But I know you and now my disciples know that you sent me."

Some say you cannot interpret the Bible as it is written. But I am told that when something is repeated over and over again in the scriptures, it is of the utmost importance. Jesus repeats that "He was sent, He is the Son of God, God is His Father, etc." Many declare that Jesus is the Son of God, and in the same breath, Jesus is God. Jesus is the Son of God. Jesus is God in the sense that He is the Word of God; the Word of God is the Son of God that came out of God the Father. God's Word is more powerful than we will ever know or even experience. Therefore, we must study it, chew it swallow it and digest it. Then, will God begin to reveal many things to us. Our problem is that we are not consistent in studying His Word, thus not giving God a chance to speak to us, let alone reveal Himself and His Son to us. Most of us Christians, according to the scriptures, have a form of godliness. We dress like Christians (some of us), we speak like Christians and we even go to church like Christian people do. However, we don't eat enough spiritual food. Without realizing it, we become spiritual sepulchers. This description fits most of our young Christians who fail to realize that there is power in the Word of God. We're not taught to study the Word of God enough. Therefore we're lacking in our spiritual growth and knowledge of Him. Our spiritual food must be a daily intake just as our natural food. Sunday school and Bible Study aren't enough. We as children of God need to study God's Word daily, beginning at an early age. Not only that, but early meaning the first part of the day. Another way of saying it is, "We are what we eat." That's why we have so many spiritual midgets instead of giants. This generation must begin to study God's Word now because it is vital for our spiritual growth. **Deuteronomy 6:6-9** cautions us to teach God's Word to our children and our children's children. Put the Word (written Word) over our doorpost and on our forehead as a way of staying in our brains, mind and thoughts. We need to be constantly reminded of what the Word of God says.

Jesus Appears to Mary after His Resurrection
Jesus Resurrection Ministry

Having faith in God that Jesus is the Christ is going to definitely help us get into heaven according to the Word of God.

John 20:17: Don't touch me until I visit the brethren and after I return to our Father God. Hallelujah. **Verse 21:** I am sending you into the world, in peace, just as my Father has sent me in peace. **Verse 31:** Believe what the prophets have written about me, that I am Christ Jesus, the Son of the true and living God. Through me, and my name you have everlasting life.

**Jesus Resurrection Ministry: Acts 1:3-7 (The book of Acts was written by Paul): After Jesus' suffering, He presented himself and gave many convincing proofs that he was alive. He appeared over a period of forty days and spoke about the Kingdom of God. On one occasion, while he was eating, he gave this command: "Do not leave Jerusalem, but wait for the gift my Father promised, which you have heard me speak about. For John baptized with water, but in a few days, you will be baptized with the Holy Spirit."

**So when they met together, his followers asked him, "Lord, are you at this time going to restore the kingdom of Israel?"

**He said to them: "It is not for you to know the times or dates the Father has set by his own authority."

***The apostolic commission*: Verses 8-9:** You will receive power when the Holy Spirit comes upon you, and you will be my witness in Jerusalem and in all Judea and in Samaria, and to the ends of the earth. After He said this, He was taken up before their very eyes, and a cloud hid him from their sight.

***The Promise of Jesus' return to earth*: Verses 10-11:** They were looking intently up into the sky as he was going, when suddenly two men dressed in white stood beside them. Men of Galilee, they said, "Why do you stand here looking into the sky? This same Jesus, whom has been taken from you into heaven, will come back in the same way you have seen him go into heaven.

Acts 2:22-28, 30-36: People of Israel, listen to this: *Jesus of Nazareth was a man accredited by God* to you by miracles, wonders and signs, which God did among you through Him, as you yourselves know. This Man (Jesus) was handed over to you by God's deliberate plan and foreknowledge, and you with the help of wicked men put Him to death by nailing him to the cross. But God raised Him from the dead, freeing Him from the agony of death, because it was impossible for death to keep its hold on Him. David said about Him in **Psalms 6:8-11, Acts 2:25 and Psalms 16:8-11:**

"I saw the Lord always before me.
because he is at my right,
I will not be shaken.
therefore my heart is glad and my
tongue rejoices;
my body will also rest in hope,
because you will not abandon me to the
realm of the dead,
you will not let you holy one see
decay
you have made known to me, the path of
of life;

you will fill me with your joy
In your presence."

Acts 2:30-35: He was a prophet (David) and knew that God had promised him an oath that He would place one of his descendants on his throne. Seeing what was to come, he spoke of the resurrection of the Messiah, that he was not abandoned to the realm of the dead, nor did his body see decay. God has raised this Jesus to life, and we all are witnesses of the fact. Exalted to the right hand of God, he has received from the Father the promised Holy Spirit and has poured out what you now see and hear. For David did not ascend to heaven, and yet he said in **Psalms 110:1 and Acts 2:34:**

> "The Lord said to my Lord,
> 'Sit at my right hand
> until I make your enemies
> A footstool for your feet.'"

Acts 2:36: Therefore let all the house of Israel know assuredly, that God has made that same Jesus, whom you have crucified, both Lord and Christ. **Acts 3:25-26:** You are the children of the prophets, and of the covenant which God made with our fathers, saying to Abraham, "And in thy seed shall all the kindred's of the earth be blessed. Unto you first God, having raised up His Son Jesus, sent Him to bless you, in turning away every one of you from his iniquities (sin).

Acts 8:33-37: In His humiliation His judgment was taken away. And who shall declare His generation? For His life is taken from the earth.

The eunuch asked Philip, "Tell me please, who is the prophet talking about? Himself or someone else?" Then Philip began with that very passage of Scripture and told him the good news about Jesus. As they traveled along the road, they came to some water, the eunuch said, "Look here is water, what can stand in the way of my being baptized?" **Verses 37-38. Philip said, "If thou believe with all thou heart, thou may." He answered and said, "I believe that Jesus Christ is the Son of God. He gave orders to stop the chariot. Then both Philip and eunuch went down into the water and Philip baptized him."

Acts 9:19-20: Saul was with the disciples in Damascus. Immediately he preached Christ in the synagogues, and that He is the Son of God.

Acts 10:34-42: Peter's sermon to the Gentiles was, "I know for sure that every nation that loves Him, and works in righteousness, is accepted with Him." The Word of God was sent to the children of Israel, preaching peace through Jesus Christ, the Lord of everyone. The Word was publicized throughout all Judea, however it began in Galilee, after John preached baptism. *God anointed Jesus of Nazareth with the Holy Ghost and with power: and Jesus went about doing good, healing all that were oppressed of the devil, for God was with Him.*

We all witness things He did, both in our country and among the Jews in Jerusalem. They slew and hanged Jesus on a tree. God raised Him up the third day and showed it in the open, not to all the people, but some so they could witnesses it to us. We ate and drank with Him after he rose from the dead. He commanded us to preach unto the people, and to testify that it is ordained of God to be the Judge of the quick and the dead.

Acts 13:28-33: Although they didn't find any reason nor cause to kill Him, yet they desired and did so. The ones that he communed with, after they fulfilled what was prophesied concerning him, they took him down form the tree, and put him in a grave. *God raised Jesus from the dead. After His resurrection, He commanded us to go into all the world, letting them know that Jesus Christ is alive, alive in us, and telling the good news and preaching the gospel and testifying to all what we've seen and heard.*

Has God done something for you? He placed His Holy Spirit in me. I know when I make my transition, I'm going back with him, for he promised if I live right, and treat others right, heaven belongs to me. Heaven is mine.

Remember three things, God can't lie, God can't die and God can't sin.

CHAPTER IX

God Judges the World through Jesus Christ

I found the Scriptures below so rich and plain (all of the Word is rich), that there was no need for anything other than what was written in the scriptures by King James. We must always remember three things: *God can't lie, God can't die and God cannot sin.*

Acts 17:24:31: God made the world and all the things in it. He is Lord of heaven and earth. He does not dwell in temples made with hands; neither is he worshiped with men's hands, as though he need help. God gives life and breath to all living things. He made all nations from one blood. Why do you think God made us? He made us for Himself. Therefore we should seek after Him, find Him and serve Him with all of our heart, might and soul. For in Him we live, move and have our being. We are made in the image of God; we are His children. Therefore, we have an inheritance with Him and in Him, we are in His will, and His plans, providing we follow in His footsteps. What more can He do? He laid the foundation, and opened up the way through His Son Jesus. We have a right to the tree of life, because He sent His only begotten Son to insure us of it. Let us not forfeit it.

Acts 17:30-31: Before Jesus physically entered this world, and shed His blood to be a sacrifice for our sins, God overlooked a lot of things in the past people did. Now that the Savior came, we have an escape through Him. He is our advocate—we have no excuse. We no longer kill animals for a sacrifice. We just repent and mean it. Be Godly sorrowful, Jesus said, then we are forgiven for our many sins, transgressions and unclean spirits.

Romans 1:10: Paul reminds us that the prophets in the Old Testament let us know that God promised us His Son Jesus, down through the linage of David, and through him, we would receive grace.

Romans 6:4: We are buried with Him by baptism into death. That like as Christ was raised up from the dead by the glory of the Father, even so we also should walk in newness of life.

Romans 8:3: The law was unable to do what Jesus Christ did for us, because it was weak in the flesh. Therefore, God sent His own Son in the likeness of sinful flesh, for our sin, and condemned sin in the flesh. So His righteousness of the law would be fulfilled in us, those that walk after the spirit and not after the flesh. *Lord God and Lord Jesus, I thank you.* **Romans 8:15-17:** Those of us who allow the spirit of God to dwell in us and lead us become joint heirs, and the children of God and His Son Jesus Christ. Then He is our Father. We're no longer slaves to sin, but free to the righteousness of God.

The Purpose of God through the Gospel

Romans 8:28-34: Nothing that happens is a surprise to God, for God is God. He knows all and see all. The Bible tells us that He knows even our thoughts way before they get to us. God knew that man was bound to sin, therefore He made a way of escape for man before the earth was formed. And that way is Jesus Christ himself, our Lord and Savior.

Jesus Christ was the first born of mankind to die the death of sin and resurrected to eternal life. Having said that, if God is for us, He is more than the entire world to us, for He so loved the world that He gave His only begotten Son, and His Son gave his life for us mortals.

Romans 10:4-9: *Christ is the end of the law for righteousness for all who believe.* Moses describes righteousness through the law. Whatever a man does is what he lives by. Now we live by grace through faith, we confess with our mouths and believe in our hearts that God has raised Jesus up from the dead. And the Word said we shall be saved—not maybe, but shall.

Romans 16:24-27: The mystery of Jesus Christ was kept a secret from the beginning of the world, but now it is made known through the scripture of the prophets of old, according to the commandment of all nations for the obedience of faith.

Protocol

(Simply put, but to the point!)

I Corinthians 11:1-3: Now, believers, I need for you to remember and keep everything in order as God has intended it to be. That is, *the head of every man is Christ; the head of the woman is the man; and the head of Christ is God.*

The Explanation

II Corinthians 1:1-5: Paul, the apostle of Jesus Christ, let us know that in following the will of God, we will suffer, but we will also get consolation and be comforted through Jesus Christ the Son of God the Father. The road gets rough sometimes, however, knowing that we have an assurance in Jesus Christ makes it easy.

II Corinthians 5:17-21: *When we get in Christ Jesus, we are different. We change our ways, habits and routines. We don't walk the same walk, nor do we talk the same talk.* We return to God as He intended for us to from the beginning through Adam. He is right there to receive us back unto Himself through His Son Jesus Christ. Now that we are new creatures, we need to spread the word that God is willing to take us back only if we believe. Believing is the most difficult for people to do. Believe that Jesus is the Son of God and that he came just to reconcile us back to his Father God. Then we will be as ambassadors for him, doing the righteousness of his Father. *Remember God made Jesus to be born in sin for us, although he didn't know any sin, that we be made the righteousness of God through him. Now we all know that God has no parts of sin. Therefore, if you read nothing else, this portion of scripture should let one know that God did not physically came down, but sent His Son, just like He said He did. As the scriptures states, God was in Christ, reconciling the world unto Himself, through His*

Son, Jesus Christ, now it is up to us to accept. Jesus Christ is the Word of reconciliation, won't you come?

II Corinthians 13:11-14: In the next few verses Paul is about to sum it all up in one lump again. Phrases such as, "The God and Father of our Lord Jesus Christ." Jesus Christ is the Son of God, Jesus emanates from God just as the Holy Spirit does. Jesus is the Word God speaks and the Holy Spirit is the power that keeps. The Word of God speaks to us and the Holy Spirit works through us. Also notice the conjunctions in the verses below, such as "and, and for." And a few more in other parts of the scriptures such as "but, yet, for, nor, and so." The Word of God comfort us and gives us confidence knowing that everything will be all right. The Word of God gives us that assurance that we have eternal life through Jesus Christ our Lord and Savior. Hearing the Word of God builds our faith in Him and strengthen us where we are weak. The Word of God builds us up where we are trodden down. The Holy Spirit of God lead us and guide us into all righteousness, truth and judgment. The Holy Spirit empowers us, teach us how and when to pray, it bears witness that we are the children of God. It reveals deep secrets, connects us to God through His Son, and helps us to be obedient to the Word of God, it bring all things to our remembrance, as well as keep us in perfect peace.

Galatians 1:1, 3-4: Jesus Christ gave himself for our many sins, just to deliver us from sin and the evils of this world. He purchased us back with his blood according to the will of God his Father, now we are heirs. **Galatians 4:1-7.** At the appointed time of God, He sent us His Son, made of a woman, under the law, to redeem all that was under the law, now we are adopted sons and daughters. Now that we are God's children, He has sent forth the spirit of His Son into our hearts, crying to Abba Father. Therefore, we are no longer servants, but sons and daughters. And I say again, that makes us heirs of God through Christ. **Ephesians 2:16-18.** To sum it all up, we can be reconciled to God through one spirit, through Jesus shedding his blood and dying on the cross, in one body that through him we have access by one spirit to the Father.

God's Plan

You will find below that Paul's writings are inevitably clear, and he makes an explicit distention between Jesus the Son, and God the Father. Both Paul and John shows these connection between God the Father and Jesus Christ as the Son of God, shown in God's Plan.

Ephesians 1:1-10 and 16-17: God has blessed us with all spiritual blessings through His Son Christ Jesus. We were chosen by God before the foundation of the world. What wisdom Paul has! God chose us to be His children and live holy, without blame before Him, in love, through His Son Jesus Christ, and having predestined us unto the adoption of children by Jesus Christ into Himself, according to the good pleasure of His will. Yes we have been redeemed through the blood of Jesus Christ for the forgiveness of our sins, according to the riches of His grace. God revealed the mystery to us, according to His will, what He had purposed in Himself. In the dispensation and when the time comes we will be gathered unto God, together in one, all things in Christ both which are in heaven and are on earth.

Verses 16-17 (the key verse is 17): *We must continue to give God praise and thanks, that the God of our Lord Jesus Christ, the Father of glory, may give unto you the spirit of wisdom and revelation in the knowledge of Him.*

Who? Jesus Christ.

Jesus Christ Over All With Power

In the following scriptures you will find that Jesus Christ was raised from the dead and sits on the right hand of his Father, God. All things are under His feet, and He is the head over all things concerning the church. Christ is exalted to be the head of the church body. God is God, all mighty, all knowing, all truth, everlasting truth, light and all power; a God through His Son, Jesus Christ, who needs no exalting. His Word is established in us, He has declared. God has put all things under the feet of Jesus Christ.

After reading the Word of God and having it sink into my spirit, I begin to wonder whether my attempt to reveal what God has shared with me would be understood. The Holy Spirit urged me to keep writing and He would do the rest.

Ephesians 1:19-23: The key to God's Word is to *believe*. The enemy is constantly trying to put doubt and discord into our spirit. To those of us who believe that Christ rose from the dead and is sitting on the right hand of God his Father, we have an inheritance with Him. **Verse 20-23:** Yes, God has raised Him from the dead and given him all power. Everything is under his auspices—the whole world and the church. Who did it? God did it. Amen.

Father God

We need to take heed to what Paul stated in **Ephesians 5:20**, giving thanks always for all things unto God and the Father in the name of our Lord Jesus Christ, for He has provided a way for our escape from the beginning of time.

God is the Father of Jesus Christ. We must go to Him through His Son. Why? Because Jesus Christ is the Word of God. We cannot do anything without having the Word of God in us. God's Word is power, knowledge, life, everlasting life, eternal life, the source of strength and salvation. Jesus Christ is the mediator between man and God.

We must recognize Jesus Christ in all that we do and say. Yes Jesus Christ's name is the one we must speak. We must honor and acknowledge him in all things. He is the Son of the living and true God; he is the Word of God. Jesus Christ is whom we need. Why? Because we need the Word, and Jesus is that Word. Where do we need the Word of God? We need the Word of God deep way down inside of us. As **Psalms 119:11** says, "The Word of God have I hid in my heart, [so] that I will not sin against God." Hallelujah!

Acts 2:21-25 and 30-36: Jesus is our salvation. Just call on his name and you shall be saved. God is speaking to Israel, America and the whole wide world. Listen to the Words of His Son—He is approved of God. He has wrought many miracles, wonders and signs that God did by him in our midst, during the days of Paul and now. Amen. **Romans 8:3, 14-17:** We couldn't get salvation through the law, it was too weak through the flesh. Therefore, God sent His own Son in the likeness of sinful flesh, and for sin, he was able to condemn sin in the flesh. This could only be done through Jesus Christ, the Son of God. Those of us who let the Spirit of God lead us become the children of God and joint heirs with His Son, Jesus Christ. It is written in the Bible, Son of God approximately 61,200,000 times, Jesus states that my Father is in heaven approximately 25,900,000 times, and that God is Jesus Christ's Father, approximately 11,400,000 times.

Jesus Praises God

Luke 10:21-24: Jesus praised his Father God. Every chance we get us to ought to give our Father God praise and glory also, constantly thanking Him for what He has done for us. Thank Him for opening our eyes to who His Son Jesus Christ is, and thank Him for His Son dying on the cross and shedding his blood for our sins, thus giving us a right to be heirs of the kingdom of God.

CHAPTER X

---∽∞∽---

The Church Mystery of Christ Revealed Through Paul Honoring God Through Jesus

(Self-explanatory Scripture Text)

Ephesians 3:2-5, 9-21: The dispensation of the grace of God has manifested to us the once-hidden mystery of Jesus Christ. Let us refer back to Genesis, when God said let us make man, the us is Jesus Christ God's Word, and the Holy Spirit that moved, who did the work. For this cause we ought to be forever grateful to our Lord and savior Jesus Christ. Giving Him glory, thanks and praise. Once again, He has made it possible for us through His suffering the right to have access to the Kingdom of God. When the world was searched no one was found worthy except for Jesus Christ.

Ephesians 5:1-5: God sent His Son Jesus which made us His dear children, now we are heirs of God and joint heirs of His Son. So we must be like Him and live a clean life free from sin and all unrighteousness. Paul named some of them: fornication, all uncleanness or covetousness, idolater, covetous, whoremonger, filthiness, nor foolish talking nor jesting, but rather giving thanks to God, just as Jesus gives thanks. Not only should we always give thanks to God in the name of Jesus Christ in sincerity, but we should constantly speak to ourselves in Psalms and hymns, making melody in our hearts to God in spiritual songs. **Ephesians 5:18-20.**

To get a better sense of Paul honoring Jesus Christ and His Father God, read **Philippians 1:1-11.**

Remember three things, God can't lie, God can't die and God can't sin.

The Sevenfold Self-Humbling and Exaltation of Christ
The Exaltation of Jesus

Philippians 2:5-11 Let us examine what it means to "let this mind be in you, which was in Christ Jesus: being in the form of God thought it not robbery to be equal with God: made himself no reputation, and took upon Him the form of a servant, and was made in the likeness of men: found in fashion as a man, humbled himself, and became obedient to death, the death of the cross." As far as I can see the mind of Jesus Christ was to be obedient to His Father God. How can we have the mind of Jesus Christ? We as mortals first believe that Jesus Christ is the Son of God. Yes, believe God. The belief is that Jesus Christ is His Son. Next, is to obey Him by loving the Lord our God with all of our soul and might, and loving our neighbor, enemy and everyone.

Verses 9-11: Does God need to exalt himself? No, He is God. People, we must recognize Jesus Christ as the Son of God, and as the Word of God. The name Christ Jesus is highly exalted above all names. The scriptures states that every knee should bow and every tongue should confess; it didn't say as the song say shall bow and confess, that Jesus Christ is Lord over all in heaven and earth.

Colossians 1:1-4, 12-19, 22, 25-26: I just love Paul's greetings and the way he addresses one in his epistles. His scholastic views just pop right out at you. He identifies himself, and not only himself, but he also let you know distinctly who Jesus the Son is and God the Father. He nails down the entire revelation of the mystery of Jesus Christ and his Father God. Paul in the New Testament and Isaiah in the Old Testament are indescribable prophets of God.

"Paul is an apostle of Jesus Christ by the will of God, and Timotheus our brother, to the saints and faithful brethren in Christ which are at Colosse: Grace be unto you and peace, from God our Father and the Lord Jesus Christ. We give thanks to God and the Father of our Lord Jesus Christ, praying always for you, since we heard of your faith in Christ Jesus."

"Give thanks to the Father, which has made us to be partakers of the inheritance of the saints in light: Who has delivered us from the power of darkness, and has translated us into the kingdom of His dear Son: In whom we have redemption through his blood, even the forgiveness of sins: Who is the image of the invisible God, the firstborn of every creature: For by him were all things created, that are in heaven, and in earth, visible and invisible, whether they be thrones, or dominions, or principalities, or powers; all things were created by him, and for him: He is before all things and by him all things consist. And he is the head of the body the church; who is the beginning, the first born from the dead that in all things he might have the preeminence. (Take a close look at the next verse, verse 19.) *For it pleased the Father that in him should all fullness dwell.*" **Verses 22, 25-26:** "In the body of his flesh through death, to present you holy and unblameable and unreproveable in his sight. Whereof I am made a minister, according to the dispensation of God which is given to me for you, to fulfill the Word of God; even the mystery which has been hid from ages and from generations, but now is made manifest to his saints."

Colossians 3:1-3, 9-10: (Will someone please, please explain this portion of scripture to me? Is God sitting on the right hand of Himself?) If you then be risen with Christ, seek those things which are above, where Christ sits on the right hand of God. To live in God is to reign with God. Love the things and ways of God, more than you do the ways and things of this world. For if we do, we will gain our justly reward according to His purpose before the world began. **II Timothy 1:1-3, 7-10.**

II Thessalonians 2:15-17: Brothers and sisters, hold on to that which you already know and have been taught, whether it be through word of mouth or script. We have something to look forward to. We know that God loves us, and has given us hope through grace. Therefore let us study God's Word according to **Deuteronomy 6.**

Remember three things, God can't lie, God can't die and God can't sin.

The Son Better Than the Prophets

Hebrew 1:1-8. *In past history God spoke to us in the Old Testament,* through His prophets, and in the New Testament through His Son Christ Jesus. Again here in Hebrew, Paul reminds us that Jesus Christ, the expressed image of God, is the one from the beginning that made the worlds has been given all power from his Father God.

CHAPTER XI

Christ High Priest After
The Order of Melchisedec

Notice in the passage of scriptures below how the apostles always included Jesus Christ with the Word "and," meaning a connection is there joining two entities together. There is no need to join the Father and Son together if the Father and the Son are the same person. Yes, they are one in agreement. There are no warring spirits between the two of them. Jesus Christ is obedient to the voice of His Father God. According to Webster's Dictionary, "and" is a joining word (a conjunction) used between two words, two phrases or two clauses.

We will find also in the following scriptures that man is made in the similitude of God, meaning a resemblance. Remember, God said to Christ, let us make man in our likeness, in our image—in other words, similar to the way we look—with a mind to think, a soul and a spirit.

God is the Father of Jesus Christ the Son. You cannot have one without the other. God is an invisible spirit. Jesus Christ is the Word, Word of God. Jesus does whatsoever the Father God tells Him to do. Jesus Christ is obedient to His Father God, from the beginning and forever.

Hebrew 5:5. *Jesus Christ didn't glorify himself to be made a high priest; but his Father God did. You are my Son, today have I begotten you.*

Although Jesus is the Son of God, He yet had to suffer in the flesh. While here on earth He prayed and made supplications with strong laments and tears

Remember three things, God can't lie, God can't die and God can't sin.

to God, the only one that could have saved Him from death. Through the suffering, pain and agony that He endured, He learned obedience. Through His obedience, He was made perfect, and through perfection came our eternal salvation. Hallelujah! Therefore God has made him the high priest forever and ever, after the order of Melchisedec.

I Peter 3:18: *Jesus Christ suffered* once for our sins, not multiple times as they did in the Old Testament, repeatedly using animals. He did for all, *the just and for the unjust, that he might bring us to God. He was put to death in the flesh, but quickened by the Holy Spirit.* He rose and ascended into heaven, and is sitting on the right of God, where everything is subject to him, waiting on that great day to meet the bride. *He received from God his Father honor and glory, heard through a voice from heaven saying, "This is my beloved Son, in whom I am well pleased." Can God say that about us? Is he pleased with our lives, the way we serve Him? Is it unto obedience, or are we doing as we please?*

I John 3:7-10: We as little children have three voices that speak to us and are always present—our voice, God's voice and the devil. If we learn to listen and play detective as to which voice we are hearing, and the one we should be listening to, we will be less prone to be deceived by the devil, and adhere to the voice of God. The Word says, "My sheep know my voice, another he will not hear." If we follow the voice of God we will then live righteous, but if we commit sin then we are sinners. Sin separates us from God. The purpose of Jesus coming from the beginning is so that we could be reborn of God, and to destroy the devil and his works. Therefore it behooves us to study God's Word, so when God speaks to us we will be able to recognize His voice and follow after righteousness. Amen.

What Happens When

We Believe and Please God

We will see in the next few passages of scripture the attributes of love being made perfect in us. Our words are so important. We must be careful in condoning things. We just could be condoning things of the devil. Jesus is the Word of God; therefore if we have Jesus, we have God.

God sanctifies us, and keeps us sanctified with His Word. The Word holds reigns on us. When we entertain a thought of disobeying God's Word, the Holy Ghost, through the Word in us, will remind us that the Word said don't commit that sin or act.

I John 3:21-24: Our commandment is that we believe in the name of Jesus Christ as the Son of God and love one another. In doing this, the Holy Spirit dwells in us.

I John 4:7-18: *God, through the book of John admonishes us to love each other. That seems to be the hardest thing for us to do. Why? I don't know. It seems like we sometimes look for reasons to dislike a person. Do we have a lack of understanding that it takes love to get us into heaven? Love is what's going to lift us up. Love is of God. God is love. God so loved the world that He gave us His only begotten Son. It doesn't matter how many children we have, we don't want to give any of them up for any reason. Yet we can't endure little things compared to what Christ suffered for our sake. Love each other regardless of what's said or done. It doesn't matter what they said nor did. Sure it hurts, Christ hurt during His suffering for us. God yet hurt when we disobey Him. Christ is yet begging our plea for our continuous transgressions. What we don't realize is that Satan's job is to plant seeds in us that will keep us out of heavens—seeds of discord, hate, unforgiving spirits, malice and so on. Not loving one will certainly keep you out. Did you know that if you don't love, you're not of God, neither are you born of God? God wants to know how can we say we love Him, having never seen Him before, yet our brothers and sisters we see every day, we don't love them? That's how you can tell that God dwells in us, by the love we have for each other. Love suffers no ill. Love covers a multitude of sin.*

I John 5:1-20: *We are overcomers of the world when we believes that Jesus is the Son of God—the one that came by water and blood, our Lord and savior, Jesus Christ. Not only by water, but water and blood. His Spirit in us bears witness because His spirit is truth. There are three that bear witness in heaven: the Father, the Word and the Holy Ghost. These three are one. And there are three that bear witness on earth: the Spirit, the water and the blood. These three agree in one also if we believe the word of man—the word of God—is greater. Therefore, we should believe God's Word of His Son. In our disbelief, we make God a liar because we don't believe the record that He left*

Remember three things, God can't lie, God can't die and God can't sin.

for us. That record is that if we have Jesus, we have eternal life, because Jesus is that eternal life.

Those that are born of God don't sin. It doesn't say we won't be tempted. I think that's where we sometimes make mistakes. Because we are tempted, we listen to the wrong voice that speaks to us and whispers that we've sinned. We sin when we yield to temptation. The Word said for us to resist the devil when he tries to seduce us to sin and he will run from us. Put the Word of God on him. But you need to study it in order to know what to say. **II John 1:3-11.** *When we abide in the Word of God, He will keep us from all transgressions. In other words, when we get in the Word, we have both God and His keeping power, a.k.a. Jesus Christ.*

Revelation 1:1-6: *John revealed Jesus as the Word of God in the book of Revelation. We need to remember that Jesus is the Word of God, the first begotten Son, and the first begotten of the dead. He is the propitiator for our sin, the prince of kings of the earth, and He in turn made us princes and kings to serve His Father God. Amen.*

Revelation 3:2-13: *Jesus wants all of us to take a spiritual look at ourselves in the mirror and strengthen our weaknesses so we can share with Him and his Father God in glory, in the great city New Jerusalem. Jesus holds the key to heaven. Only He can open and close the door. The door is open to the ones who love and obey Him, and closed to the ones who worship the devil and refuse to repent. Lord God I want to be among those who enter your gates of heaven.*

CHAPTER XII

Scriptures that Reveal
CHRIST'S DIVINITY AND CHRIST CALLED GOD

Matthew 1:22-23: All the things that were prophesied by the prophets of old, that Jesus would be born of a virgin, and God with us, was fulfilled in the New Testament.

John 1:1, John 10:33: The Jews could not believe that Jesus was the Son and the Word of God. If we can believe, we can conceive that when the Bible reads that in the beginning was the Word, the Word was with God and the Word was God, meaning that it is God's Word, and His Word was with Him. And He sent His Word out from Him, manifest in the flesh. It was a hard thing for the Jews to understand. Therefore they doubted and sought to kill him for making himself equal with God. **John 20:28.**

Acts 20:28: I thank God for Jesus, for He purchased the church back with His own blood, to redeem us, the wayward children, for his Father God.

I Timothy 3:16: The great mystery of godliness: God was manifest in the flesh, justified in the Spirit, seen of angels, preached to the Gentiles, believed in the world and received up to glory.

I John 1:1-2: *From the beginning we have heard, seen with our eyes, looked on, and touched with our hands the Word of life. For the life was manifested, and we have seen it and bear witness and show to you the eternal life which was with the Father and was manifested to us.*

I John 5:20: "We know that the Son of God is come, and has given us understanding, that we may know him that is true, and we are in him that is true, even in his Son Jesus Christ. This is the true God, and eternal life."

Isaiah 9:6: "For unto us a child is born, unto us a son is given, and the government shall be upon his shoulder: and his name shall be called Wonderful, Counselor, The Mighty God, The everlasting Father the Prince of Peace."

Scriptures that Reveal
JESUS MADE EQUAL WITH GOD

John 3:35: *The Father loves the Son, and has given all things into his hand.* **John 5:23:** *That all men should honor the Son, even as they honor the Father. He that honor not the Son honors not the Father.* **John 10:30:** *I and my Father are one.*

John 12:44-45: *Jesus cried and said, He that believes on me, believes not on me, but on him that sent me. And he that sees me sees him that sent me.*

John 14:7-9, and 11: *If you had known me, you should have known the Father also: and from henceforth you know him, and have seen him. Phillip said unto Lord, show us the Father, and it suffices us. Jesus said unto him, "Have I been so long time with you, and yet has thou not known me, Phillip? He that has seen me has seen the Father; and how you say then show us the Father? Believe me that I am in the Father and the Father in me: or else believe me for the very works' sake."*

John 15:23-24: *He that hated me hated my Father also. If I had not done among them the works which none other man did, they had not had sin: but now have they both seen and hated both me and my Father.*

John 17:10, 21-23: "Jesus said to his Father, all mine are yours, and yours are mine; and I am glorified in them. That they all may be one; as you, Father, are in in me, and I in you, that they also may be one in us: that the world may believe that you have sent me. The glory which you gave me, I have given them; that they may be one, even as we are one. I in them and you in me, that they may be made perfect in one; and that the world may know that you sent me, and has loved them as you has loved me."

Philippians 2:6: Jesus, being in the form of God, thought it not robbery to be equal with God. **Colossians 1:15, 19:** Who is the image of the invisible God, the firstborn of every creature: For it pleased the Father that in him should all fullness dwell. **Colossians 2:9:** For in him dwells all the fullness of the God bodily. **I John 2:23:** Whosoever denies the Son, the same has not the Father: (but) he that acknowledges the Son has the Father also. **Matthew 11:27:** All things are delivered to me of my Father: and no man knows the Son, but the Father; neither knows any man the Father, save the Son, and he to whomsoever the Son will reveal him. **John 5:17-18:** But Jesus answered them, my Father works hitherto, and I work. *Therefore the Jews sought the more to kill him, because he not only had broken the Sabbath, but said also that God was his Father, making himself equal with God.* **John 10:33, 36-38:** *The Jews answered him saying, for good work we stone thee not; but for blasphemy; and because that you, being a man, make thyself God. Say ye of him, whom the Father has sanctified, and sent into the world, thou blasphemes; because I said, I am the Son of God? If I do not the works of my Father, believe me not. But if I do, though you believe not me, believe the works: that you may know, and believe, that the Father is in me and me in Him.* **John 17:5:** *Now, O Father, glorify thou me with thine own self with the glory which I had with thee before the world was.*

Scriptures that Reveal
JESUS PERFORMING THE WORKS OF GOD

John 1:3, 10: *All things were made by him; and without him was not anything made that was made. He was in the world, and the world was made by him, and the world knew him not.*

Ephesians 3:9: *I Paul, want to make sure that all men see what is the fellowship of every mystery, which from the beginning of the world has been hid in God, who created all things by Jesus Christ.* **Colossians 1:16:** *For* *by him were all things created, that are in heaven, and that are in the earth, visible and invisible, whether they be thrones, or dominions, or principalities, or powers: all things were created by him, and for him.*

Hebrew 1:10: *You Lord, in the beginning has laid the foundation of the earth; and the heavens are the works of your hands.* **Revelations 3:14:** *To the angel of the church of the Laodicea's write; these things said the Amen, the faithful and true witness, the beginning of the creation of God.* **Psalms 102:25:** *Of old has you laid the foundation of the earth: and the heavens are the work of your hands.* **I Corinthians 8:6:** *But to us is but one God, the Father, of whom are all things, and we in him: and we by him.*

Scriptures that Reveal
JESUS CALLED THE SON OF GOD

Mark 1:1: The beginning of the gospel of Jesus Christ, the Son of God; **Mark 9:7:** There was a cloud that overshadowed them: and a voice came out of the cloud, saying, "This is my beloved Son: hear him." **Luke 1:35:** Therefore also that holy thing which shall be born of thee shall be called the Son of God. **John 5:17-18:** "But Jesus answered them, "My Father works hereto, and I work." Therefore the Jews sought the more to kill him, because he not only had broken the Sabbath, but also said that God was his Father, making him equal with God. **John 8:19, 38:** Then said they unto him, where is thy Father? Jesus answered, "You neither know me, nor my Father: if you had known me, you would have known my Father also. I speak that which I have seen with my Father; and ye do that which you have seen with your father." **John 10:36:** Say ye of him, whom the Father have sanctified, and sent into the world, thou blasphemes; because I said, I am the Son of God? **John 17:25:** O righteous Father, the world has not known thee, and these have known that thou has sent me.

Galatians 4:4: When the fullness of the time was come, God sent forth His Son, made of a woman under the law. **Ephesians 3:14-15:** For this cause I bow my knees unto the Father of our Lord Jesus Christ, of whom the whole family in heaven and earth is named. **Hebrew 1:2:**

The prophets has in these days spoken unto us by his Son, whom He appointed heir of all things by whom also He made the worlds.

Hebrew 3:5-6: Moses verily was faithful in all his house as a servant, for a testimony of those things which were to be spoken after; but Christ as a Son over his own house; whose house are we, if we hold fast the confidence and the rejoicing of the hope firm unto the end. **Hebrew 5:5, 8:** *Also Christ glorified not himself to be made a high priest; but He that said unto Him, "Thou art my Son, today have I begotten thee. Though He were a Son, yet taught He obedience by the things which He suffered. I **John 4:15:** Whosoever shall confess that Jesus is the Son of God, God dwell in him and him in God? I **John 5:5:** Who is he that overcomes the world, but he that believes that Jesus is the Son of God? Psalms 2:7, 12: Kiss the Son, less He be angry and you perish from the way, when His wrath is kindled but a little. Blessed are all they that put their trust in Him. **Psalms 89:27:** Also I will make him my firstborn, higher than the kings of the earth. **Matthew 3:17:** "Lo a voice from heaven, saying, "This is my beloved Son, in whom I am well pleased."*

Mark 13:32: Of that day and that hour knows no man, no, not the angels which are in heaven, *neither the Son, but the Father.* **Luke 10:22:** *All things are delivered to me of my Father: and no man knows who the Son is, but the Father: and who the Father is, but the Son, and he to whom the Son will reveal him.*

John 1:14, 18: The Word was made flesh and, dwelt among us, (and we beheld his glory, the glory as of the only begotten of the Father,) full of grace and truth. *No man has seen God at any time; the only begotten Son, which is in the bosom of the Father, He has declared Him.*

Acts 3:13: The God of Abraham, and of Isaac, and of Jacob, the God of our fathers, has glorified His Son Jesus; whom you delivered up, and denied Him in the presence of Pilate, when he was determined to let Him go. **Romans 5:10:** *For if, when we were enemies, we were reconciled to God by the death of His Son, much more, being reconciled, we shall be saved by His life.*

Hebrew 1:5: For unto which of the angels said he at any time, thou art my Son, this day have I begotten thee. **Revelation 2:18:** Unto the angel of the church in Thyatira write; these things said the Son of God, who has His eyes like unto a flame of fire, and His feet are like brass. The Bible reveals that Jesus was called the Son of God approximately 12,500,000 times and Jesus said I am the Son of God approximately 14,400,000 times.

Scriptures that Reveal
JESUS RAISING THE DEAD

John 5:21, 25, 28-29: For as the Father raise up the dead, quickens them; even so the Son quickens whom he will. Very, very I say unto you, the hour is coming, and now is, when the dead shall hear the voice of the Son of God: and they that hear shall live. Marvel not at this: for the hour is coming, in the all that are in the graves shall hear His voice; and shall come forth; they that have done good, unto the resurrection of life; and they have done evil, unto the resurrection of damnation. All will rise and go to their destination, whether it be heaven or hell. **John 11:25:** Jesus said unto her, I am the resurrection, and the life: he that believes in me, though he were dead, yet shall he live. **Philippians 3:21:** Who shall change our vile body that it may be fashioned like unto the glorious body, according to the working whereby he is able even to subdue all things? **John 6:40:** This is the will of Him that sent me, that everyone which sees the Son, and believes on Him may have everlasting life: and I will raise Him up at the last day.

Scriptures that Reveal
JESUS JUDGING THE WORLD

Matthew 7:22: Many will say in that day, Lord, Lord, have we not prophesied in thy name? And in thy name have cast out devils? And in thy name done many wonderful works?

Matthew 16:27: The Son of man shall come in the glory of His Father with his angels; and then He shall reward every man according to His works.

Matthew 24:30: Then shall appear the sign of the Son of man in heaven: and then shall all the tribes of the earth mourn, and they shall see the Son of man coming in the clouds of heaven with power and great glory.

Matthew 25:31: When the Son of man shall come in His glory, and the holy angels with Him, then shall He sit upon the throne of His glory.

John 5:22, 27: *The Father judges no man, but has committed all judgment to the Son: And has given Him authority to execute judgment also, because He is the Son of man.* **John 8:15-16:** *You judge after the flesh: I judge no man. And yet if I judge, my judgment is true, for I am not alone, but I and the Father that sent me.*

Acts 10:42: He commanded us to preach unto the people, and to testify that is He which was ordained of God to be the judge of quick and dead. **Romans 2:16:** In the day when God shall judge the secrets of men by Jesus judgment seat of Christ. **II Corinthians 5:10:** For we must all appear before the judgment and seat of Christ; that everyone may receive things done in His body, according to that He has does, whether it be good or bad, we will be judged accordingly. **II Timothy 4:1:** I charge thee therefore before God, and the Lord Jesus Christ, who shall judge the quick and the dead at His appearing and His kingdom.

Revelation 1:7: Behold, He comes with clouds; and every eye shall see Him, and they also which pierced Him: and all kindred's of the earth shall wail because of Him. **Revelations 22:12:** Behold I come quickly; and my reward is with me, to give every man according as his work shall be. **Acts 17:31:** Because He has appointed a day in which He will judge the world in righteousness by that man whom He has ordained: whereof He has given assurance unto all men, in that He has raised Him from the dead.

Remember three things, God can't lie, God can't die and God can't sin.

CHAPTER XIII

Scriptures Declaring Jesus Christ as Lord

Matthew 12:8: The Son of man is Lord of the Sabbath day. **Mark 2:28, Luke 6:46:** Why call me Lord, Lord, and do not the things which I say?

Matthew 22:41-45 and Luke 20:41-44: While the Pharisees were gathered together Jesus asked them, "What do you think of Christ? Whose Son is he?" They *said unto Him, the Son of David. He said unto them how* does David in the Spirit call Him Lord, saying, The Lord said unto my Lord, sit thou on my right hand, till I make thine enemies thy footstool? If David then calls Him Lord, how is He His Son? He shall be called the Son of the Highest; and the Lord God shall give unto him the throne of his father David: and he shall reign over the house of Jacob forever; and of his kingdom there shall be no end.

John 13:13: You call me Master and Lord: and you say well: for so I am. **Acts 10:36:** The Word which God sent unto the children of Israel; preaching peace by Jesus Christ. (*He is Lord of all!*) **Romans 14:9:** For to this end Christ both died, and rose, and revived, that He might be Lord of both the dead and the living. **I Corinthians 2:8:** None of the princes of this world knew: for had they known it, they would not have crucified the Lord of glory. **Galatians 1:3:** Grace be to you, and peace, from God the Father, and from our Lord Jesus.

Galatians 6:18: Brethren, the grace of our Lord Jesus Christ by with your spirit. **Ephesians 1:22:** He has put all things under His feet, and gave Him to be the head over all things to the church. **Philippians 2:11:** Every tongue should confess that Jesus Christ is Lord, to the glory of

God the Father. **II Thessalonians 2:16-17:** Now our Lord Jesus Christ Himself and God, even our Father, which has loved us, and has given us everlasting consolation and good hope through grace. Comfort your hearts, and establish you in every good word and work. **I Timothy 6:14:** That thou keep this commandment without spot, without rebuke, until the appearing of our Lord Jesus Christ. **Hebrew 2:3, 8:** How shall we escape, if we neglect so great salvation; which at the first began to be spoken by the Lord, and was confirmed unto about them that heard Him; thou shall put all things in subjection under His feet. For in that He put all in subjection under Him, He left nothing that is not put under him. But now we see not yet all things put under Him.

II John 3: Grace be with you, mercy and peace from God the Father, and from the Lord Jesus Christ, the Son of the Father, in truth and love. **Revelations 1:20:** You saw in my right hand and the seven golden candle sticks. The seven stars are angels of the seven churches and the seven candle sticks which you saw are the seven churches.

Other Scriptures Where Jesus is Called Lord

Revelation 2:1, 12, 16 and 18
Revelation 3:1
Revelation 14:14
Revelation 17:14
Revelation 19:21
Jeremiah 23:6
Matthew 28:6
Mark 5:19-20
Luke 5:8
Acts 2:36
I Corinthians 8:6
Hebrew 1:10
I Timothy 6:15
Titus 1:4

Revelation 19:11-16: I saw heaven opened, behold a white horse; and He that sat upon Him was called Faithful and True, and in righteousness He do judge and make war. His eyes were a flame of fire, and on His head were many crowns; and He had a name written, that no man knew, but He Himself. And He was clothed with a vesture dipped in blood: and his name is called *"The Word of God"*. And the armies which were in heaven followed Him upon white horses, clothed in fine linen, white and clean, out of His mouth goes a sharp sword that with it He should smite the nations; and He shall rule them with a rod of iron: and He treads the wine press of the fierceness and wrath of Almighty God. And He has on His vesture and on His thigh a name written *King of Kings and Lord of Lords.*

Scriptures showing
Christ Possessing the Attributes of God

(Eternal)
John 1:2
John 3:13
John 5:26
John 8:56-58
John 13:3
John 16:28
John 17:5, 24
Acts 3:15
I Corinthians 15:47-49
Revelation 1:17-18
John 1:1
Hebrews 1:11-12
Hebrews 13:8
I Timothy 6:16
Revelation 1:8

(Omnipresent)
Matthew 18:20
Matthew 28:20
Ephesians 1:23
John 3:13
Hebrews 1:3

(Omniscient)
Matthew 9:4
Matthew 12:25
Mark 2:8
Luke 6:8
Luke 9:47
John 2:24-25
John 5:42
John 6:64
John 10:15
John 16:30

(Omnipotent)
Matthew 28:18
John 10:17-18

(Unchangeable)
Hebrews 1:11-13

(Sinless)
John 7:18
John 8:29, 50
Romans 15:3
I Peter 2:22-23
Hebrews 1:9
I John 3:5

(In Power)
Matthew 20:23
John 5:19, 30

(In Goodness)
Matthew 9:16-17

(In Knowledge)

Mark 13:32: *That day and that hour knows no man, no, not the angels which are in heaven, neither the Son, but the Father.* **John 3:34:** *Whom God*

Remember three things, God can't lie, God can't die and God can't sin.

has sent speaks the words of God: for God gives not the Spirit by measure unto Him. **John 5:20:** *For the Father loves the Son, and shows Him all things that Himself does: and He will show Him greater works than these that you may marvel.* **John 8:26, 28:** *I have many things to say and to judge of you: but He that sent me is true; and I speak to the world those things which I have heard of Him.* **Verse 28:** *Jesus said to them, "When you have lifted up the Son of man, then shall you know that I am He, and that I do nothing of myself; but as my Father has taught me, I speak these things.* **John 12:49-50:** *For I have not spoken of myself; but the Father which sent me, He gave me a commandment, what I should say, and what I should speak.* **Verse 50:** *And I know his commandment is life everlasting: whatsoever I speak therefore, even as the Father said unto me, so I speak.*

John 15:15: *Henceforth I call you not servants; for the servant knows not what his lord does: but I have called you friends; for all things that I have heard of my Father I have made known to you.* **John 16:15:** *All things that the Father has are mine: therefore said I, that He shall take of mine, and shall show it unto you.*

Scripture Revealing

Christ in His Kingly Character Opening the Book
and
Marriage to the Lamb

Revelation 5:5-10: One of the elders said unto me, weep not: behold, the Lion of the tribe of Juda, the Root of David, has prevailed to open the book, and to loose the seven seals thereof. And I beheld, and lo, in the midst of the throne and of the four beasts, and in the midst of the elders, stood a Lamb as it had been slain, having seven horns and seven eyes, which are the seven spirits of God sent forth into all the earth. And he came and took the book out of the right hand of Him that sat upon the throne. And when he had taken the book, the four beasts and four and twenty elders fell down, before the Lamb having every one of them harps, and golden vials full of odors, which are prayers of saints. And they sung a new song, saying, thou art worthy to take the book, and to open the seals thereof: for thou was slain, and has redeemed us to God by thy blood out of every kindred, and tongue, and people, and nation;

and has made us unto our God kings and priests; and we shall reign on the earth.

To Summarize

From A Theological Point of View on "Is Jesus God?"

Is Jesus and God the same Person or are they separate? This is a universal question which has been dealt with by man in many different ways, religions, theologians, and beliefs, including the early church. The intent of this book was to polarize the truth as I view it through the eye of the Word of God and other Theologians. My chief aim was to explore and investigate the gospel as evidence that Jesus is the Son of God.

In my search for the truth, "Is Jesus God?", or God Himself posing as Jesus? It was found in twenty-one chapters, and six different books of the Bible, referring to Jesus as The Son of God, by D. Guthre and other theologians.

In Genesis 1:26, "God said let US (Father, Son, and Holy Spirit), make mankind in OUR image, after OUR likeness and let them have complete authority over the creation of the earth. The fact that the plural form was used meaning more than one, gives us an indication that it was more than ONE. If God and Jesus is the same entity (only one) why use plurals? God is highly intelligent. His intelligence is beyond measures, especially ours. Therefore, it would be something wrong with this grammatical statement. If there are three which bear witness in Heaven, how can we arrive at ONE? In Isaiah 9:6, states "For to us a Child is born, to us a Son is given; and the government shall be upon His shoulders, and His name shall be called Wonderful Counselor, Mighty God, Everlasting Father (of Eternity), Prince of Peace".

Other findings of theological expressions: God Himself is three in one. It states that, "in a very real way God is a Community and exists in a relationship with Himself. (Nelson, p. 7)

In the New Testament, Jesus spoke as God the Father did in numerous occasions, in the Old Testament. Jesus spoke in reference to God as His

Heavenly Father 51 times in the New Testament. This evidence alone indicates that Jesus highly recognized God as His Father, and that His Father sent Him on a special mission.

Matthew, Mark, Luke and John recorded the application of the title Son of God to Jesus. They recognized the fact that Jesus came from God, and had a special relationship to God. Another link used, is Jesus the Messiah? Matthew 26:63, Caiaphas, puts the direct question, "Tell us if you are the Christ, the Son of God?" (Mark has, Son of the Blessed, and Luke splits the question in two). In all accounts, Jesus is in the affirmative with sufficient clarity. Luke 4:41, also links the Son of God with the Messiah, where the demons even recognize Jesus as the Son of God. (Guthrie, pp. 305-6)

The debate during Jesus stay here on earth was, who is this man called Jesus? Some say a prophet, other say John the Baptist and some Elias. Theologically speaking, Son of Man is understood as a title of Majesty. It also points out through research, that the Divine Majesty of Jesus and His ultimate oneness with God, and His Obedience to His Father. (Cullman, p. 270)

Did Jesus understand Himself to be the "Son of God?" Through this investigation, the early church first viewed Jesus as the Son of God, under the influence of the Old Testament, without Jesus Himself giving Himself this name. Whether Jesus called Himself Son of God or not, according to the witness of the whole gospel tradition, "the Son of God", title as applied to Jesus, expresses the historical and qualitative uniqueness of His relation to His Father". (Cullman, p, 275)

In Matthew 26:63, (during the early church), the worst was brought out in the chief priest, elders and council. They looked for false witness to testify against Jesus, so He could be denounced and put to death. However, they wanted Jesus to make the statement Himself, that He was the Christ, the Son of God.

Jesus being the Son of God caused the earth to quake. Only then did they begin to realize that Jesus was truly the Son of God.

Finally through the eyes of theologians, Paul recognizes the Father and Son relationship in I Corinthians 15:20-28. For He (the Father) has put all things under His (Christ's) feet. But when it says all things are put under subjection (under Him), it is evident that He (Himself) is expected who does the subjecting of all things to Him. However, when everything is subjected to Him, then the Son Himself will also subject Himself to (the Father) who put all things under Him, so that God may be all in all (be everything to everyone, supreme, the indwelling and controlling factor of life." (Zondervan, p. 1739, ch. 15, vs. 27-28)

The Conclusion Yet The Beginning Is Jesus God?

I have studied the scriptures, kept the faith and I remain that Jesus Christ is the Son of God. Jesus Christ is the Word of God. The Word is the Son and the Son is the Word. Jesus Christ was visible in the flesh, but no one has ever seen God. God is a Spirit, and we must worship Him in spirit and in truth. Only Jesus Christ His Son has seen Him. Jesus Christ was from the beginning hid in the bosom of God. When Jesus Christ spoke to God, He always recognized Him as Father. And when God spoke to Jesus He always used the word Son. Jesus always gave recognition and credit to His Father God. And God always found satisfaction and glory in His Son, Jesus Christ. God the Father and Jesus Christ the Son are one in agreement; they are not separate, just like we and our voice and spirit aren't separate from us. In **Revelation 19:13** remember that Jesus' name is called, "The Word of God."

There's no greater authority than our Lord God Himself, our Creator, through Jesus Christ, the Son of God, the propitiator, for us all. No limits are in Him. One portion of scripture asks is there anything too hard for God? The answer is no. Our thinking is so limited. Our intellect does not exceed that of our God; neither does it match. God said, "My ways are not you ways, neither are my thoughts your thoughts." So why do we try to reduce God down to our little minds and pea brains? We can't even begin to use our imagination towards our God. We can only see the minute portion, a glimpse that He allows us to see. Our minds would explode if it were to contain the many thoughts of our God. The little knowledge He allows us to have is so small compared to that of our God Almighty. God shared with me this morning that throughout the Old Testament, He constantly mentions both He and His Son Jesus Christ when speaking to the prophets. For example, when He speak of His Son Jesus Christ, it's termed as listen to the Word of the Lord, when speaking of Himself, it states thus said the Lord God. Ezekiel is a good example of that.

John 5:22: The Father (God) judges no man, but has committed all judgment unto the Son: That all men should honor the Son, even as they honor the Father. He that doesn't honor the Son, does not honor the Father, which sent Him.

God sent two things into the earth for us that are a part of Him—one the Holy Spirit (the Holy Ghost) and two, His Word (Jesus Christ).

Finally, in **Deuteronomy 30:11-16, and 19-20** is the commandment given to us through the Word, which is to love the Lord our God, walk upright in His ways, keep His commandments, statues, and judgments so we can live eternally, and bring others to Him. Do this and God will bless us in all of our endeavors wherever we go. When we decide to obey God, we choose life for both we ourselves and our seeds. But when we disobey, we are choosing death. It is up to us to make the choice. We can number our days now on earth to be long or short. We also can chose our destiny for the future—to either spend eternity in heaven or hell. **I John 5:11-13.**

Revelation 22:13: I am the Alpha and the Omega, the beginning and the ending, the first and the last. Jesus Christ, the Word of God, is one of the Attributes of God, just like the Holy Ghost is an Attribute of God. *Amen.*

EPILOGUE

In the Old Testament, the first Adam, God spoke and cursed the people because of sin. In the New Testament, the second Adam, God spoke and blessed the people with forgiveness of sin through our Lord and savior Jesus Christ.

Some say that we worship three Gods, but we don't, we worship one God. In Him, is God the Father, God the Son, and God the Holy Ghost? God is the God of all, without Him, there is nothing—one Lord, one faith and one baptism. God is an invisible Spirit. The attributes of God are the Word of God, which is Jesus Christ, and the Holy Ghost or Holy Spirit, which is the keeping power of God that keeps us from sinning. You need the Holy Spirit of God because it fills you with knowledge and understanding. The Spirit of God is not something to just jerk you around or be in an emotional state of being, but to give one love, peace, understanding and the ability to do things through the supernatural power of God (such as supernatural healing power). The Spirit gives power to open blind eyes that never experienced seeing before so now they can see; or the supernatural ability to read, write and spell, although you never went to school nor were you taught. We must allow His spirit to enter inside of us by receiving the Holy Ghost, the keeper, to seal the Word of God inside of us. I am a witness that the Holy Spirit leads you, guides you, protects you and teaches you. We must develop that spiritual ear to be able to hear and recognize the Holy Spirit, when it's speaking to us.

As I said earlier, just like we accept the Holy Ghost as a part that comes from God, without any difficulty, we need to accept the Word of God, which is Jesus Christ, without any difficulty as well. They both emanate from God.

There's no greater authority than our Lord God Himself, our Creator. It is through Jesus Christ, the Son of God, and the propitiator for us all, that our sins are forgiven. God is the one and only true living God. I said this before, but I'm going to say it again, near verbatim: *No limits are in God. "Is there anything too hard for God?" The answer is no. Our thinking is so limited. Our intellect will never exceed that of our God, nor does it match. God said, "My ways are not your ways; my thoughts are not your thoughts." So why do we try to reduce God down to our weak little minds. We can't even begin to use our imagination towards our God. We can only see a minute portion, a glimpse, which He allows us to see. Our minds would explode if it were to contain the many thoughts of our God.* The little knowledge He empowers us with is so small compared to God almighty. So why do some say that God came down, when He declares that He sent His Son—meaning, He sent His Word, which is His Son, Jesus Christ? Are you saying God can't have a Son? Is it impossible for God to have a Son? God doesn't need sex to have a Son. So what are you saying? He formed Adam out of the soil, and Eve out of Adam's side. God is everything we are and more. He made us in His image, didn't He? Whatever He declares, it is so. Therefore, He does have a Son, and His name is Jesus Christ, and Jesus Christ is the Word of God. Jesus Christ declares that His name is "The Word of God" in the book of Revelation.

I often reminisce concerning the greatness of our God, knowing that He is not a God of recycle, but the God of creation, the originator of every and all things that are here, that are to come, that are the visible and invisible, and that are known and the unknown. Every time a human being is born, He gives them a new set of teeth, ears, hands, feet and our own fingerprints. These prints are never duplicated; there never has been a mistake in the identity of our prints. Our entry into this world, He breathes His breath into us, when our transition time comes, His oxygen leaves our bodies. We were made from dirt. Can we make flesh or anything that can live from dirt? The answer is no. We can't do anything but accept whatever God has given us. When we die, we will return to being dirt. God sends the snow, rain, sunshine and the four seasons when He wants, and in the amount He desires. We have absolutely no control of when, where or what the amount will be. All we can do is accept whatever God does.

This is the greatest one to me: Every day that God allows us to awake, we wake up to a brand new day. We can't move the day forward, nor can we move it backward. It is the day the Lord has made; all we can do is rejoice and be glad. I have spent many years just thinking about our wonderful God and His beautiful skies, decorated with the moon, stars, sun and the beautiful array of clouds. What amazes me about them is that they never need repair, in all these billions of years. He is *awesome*. I can't find words to describe Him.

God did all of that, and yet He, Himself, came down to earth to die for our sins? No, He did not. He sent His Son, His Word, to be that sacrificial offering, up to Him, as a sweet-smelling savior, Jesus Christ. There was no sin in Him, for He could not sin, because He is the Word of God. Jesus Christ came to clean up what we messed up through the first Adamic Covenant.

I found Him in **Genesis 14:18** to be the Most High God. In Exodus chapter three He is the great *I am that I am*, my name is *I am*. God's name can be whatever He deems it to be. He is God. He made the names. He created the languages. We see in **Genesis 11:1** that God created the different languages, and not only that, He speaks all of the languages. *Hallelujah*. From the beginning, God so wanted His Word to be inside of us and in our hearts, souls and minds. We see this when He spoke to Moses in Deuteronomy, instructing us how to get His Word in us, for keeps, and as a reminder when we are sometimes tempted. He told us to write them over the door post, put them as frontlets on our foreheads, write them on the walls, and teach them to our children and our children's children. Then He gave us his Son in the New Testament, which is the Word of God, spoken about in the Old Testament, the book of Isaiah. He gave us the Holy Ghost, the keeping power, the sealer, to keep the Word, Jesus Christ, in us. He gave us a scripture to read like this, "For God so loved the world, that He gave His only begotten Son, that whosoever believe in Him shall not perish, but have everlasting life." He then told us to let the mind that was in Christ Jesus live in us as well.

With all the laws, decrees and commandments, which is approximately 613, or maybe even more, Jesus Christ narrowed all of them in the Old Testament, to hang on these two, in the New Testament: love the Lord thy God with all thy heart, soul, strength and mind, and love thy neighbor as thy self. And if we do this, we have kept the Word of God and we shall live forever, for we will have kept the commandments of our Lord and savior.

He's the author and finisher of all things and everything. We as a people are the children of God. We need to listen with our spiritual ear and obey the voice of God. I like what God said to Moses when he tried to wiggle out of leading the Israelites due to his speech impediment. He asked Moses, "Who made man's mouth?" Then, He instructed Moses to go, and He (God) would teach him and put the words in his mouth. Let us go, and let God put His Word in our mouths, in our hearts, in our souls and in our minds. We must learn to recognize the voice of God and obey it by living it and going out and telling it on the mountaintops, over the hills and everywhere, that Jesus Christ has come. The Word of God is here; receive it, chew it up, digest it, open up, let Him in and spread His Word. *The good news of God is everywhere. Praise God, Amen.*

We believe that God spoke everything into existence, or don't we? When He spoke, He did it through His Son Jesus Christ. Jesus Christ was right there with His Father God in the book of Genesis. That's what He said in the Holy Scriptures. "Father, I would that you glorify me, with your own self, the way I had with you before the world was." Jesus spoke these words in **John 17:5**, referring to His relationship with his Father in Genesis, before and during creation. Another nugget is found in **John 16:28** when Jesus said He came forth, from His Father, into the world, and He was returning back to heaven, to His Father.

I John 1:1 states, "That which was from the beginning, we have seen, heard, and touched Him." The beginning of the books of the Bible is Genesis. Jesus Christ was right there in the beginning as the Word of Life. The last is Revelation, where Jesus said "I am Alpha, the beginning, the first, and Omega, the last, and the end."

According to Paul, in **Corinthians 15:28**, Jesus Christ and the Holy Ghost both are subject unto God. God has put everything under Christ. All things are subdued under Him. The order is like this, God is the head of Jesus, Jesus is the head of the church, and the husband is the head over the wife. We all are the children of God.

Paul in **Colossians 1:3 and 15:** *Give thanks to God, the Father of our Lord Jesus Christ, who is the image of the invisible God, the first born of every creature. To me, it just doesn't get any clearer. This explains, "When you've seen me, you've seen the Father." God wasn't born, and neither can He die. We cannot figure God out. If we could, would He be God?*

Revelations 22:13: *"I am the alpha and Omega, the beginning and the ending, the first and the last." Jesus Christ, the Word of God, is one of the Attributes of God, just like the Holy Ghost is an Attribute of God. First God, second Jesus Christ and third the Holy Ghost. AMEN.*

Revelation 19:7-16: *I conclude that His name is "THE WORD OF GOD." And He is crowned "KING OF KINGS AND LORD OF LORDS." AMEN AGAIN.*

BIBLIOGRAPHY

Cullman, O., *The Christology of the New Testament, Philadelphia, Pennsylvania, Westminster 1963.*

Erickson, M.J., *Man Needs and God's Gift, Grand Rapids, Michigan, Baker Book House 1975.*

Erickson, M.J., *Man Needs and God's Gift, Grand Rapids, Michigan, Baker Book House 1976.*

Erickson, M.J., *Christian Theology, Grand Rapids, Rapids, Michigan, Volume I., 1984.*

Guthrie, D., *New Testament Theology, Downers Grove, Illinois, Inter-Varsity, 1981.*

Nelson, Thomas, *The Word In Life Study Bible, KJV, Nashville, Tennessee, Thomas Nelson Inc. 1996.*

Zondervan, *The Amplified Bible, LaHabra, California, Zondervan Corporation, 1987.*

Remember three things, God can't lie, God can't die and God can't sin.

Printed in the United States
By Bookmasters